Parker Gillmore

All Round the World

Adventures in Europe, Asia, Africa, and America

Parker Gillmore

All Round the World
Adventures in Europe, Asia, Africa, and America

ISBN/EAN: 9783744760744

Printed in Europe, USA, Canada, Australia, Japan

Cover: Foto ©ninafisch / pixelio.de

More available books at **www.hansebooks.com**

ALL ROUND THE WORLD.

Adventures in Europe, Asia, Africa, and America.

BY PARKER GILLMORE,

"UBIQUE."

AUTHOR OF 'GUN, ROD, AND SADDLE;' 'ACCESSIBLE FIELD SPORTS,' &c. &c. &c.

WITH ILLUSTRATIONS

BY SIDNEY P. HALL.

LONDON:
CHAPMAN AND HALL, 193, PICCADILLY.
1871.

CONTENTS.

CHAP.		PAGE
I.	BOYHOOD AND MISCHIEF	1
II.	MY FIRST STEEPLECHASE	16
III.	A RUN WITH THE GIBRALTAR FOXHOUNDS	29
IV.	RAMBLES IN SPAIN	39
V.	BARBARY FIELD SPORTS	47
VI.	AFLOAT IN THE MEDITERRANEAN AND ASHORE IN NORTH AFRICA	61
VII.	AN INDIAN HUNTING ENCAMPMENT	67
VIII.	FIRST BLOOD	75
IX.	A SHARP BURST	82
X.	THE STORM	88
XI.	A VETERAN BOAR	95
XII.	THE SEARCH FOR THE MURDERER	105
XIII.	THE TIGER'S DEATH	113
XIV.	A FOREST SCENE	120
XV.	CATCHING A SHARK	125
XVI.	TRICKING AN ALLIGATOR	131
XVII.	FAST ON A CORAL REEF	138
XVIII.	A BATTLE IN A BILLIARD ROOM	143
XIX.	CHASED BY A BUFFALO	149
XX.	AMONG CHINESE PIRATES	157
XXI.	SHOOTING NEAR HONG KONG	164
XXII.	DRIFTING TO DEATH	175

Chap.		Page
XXIII.	Wild Duck Shooting	183
XXIV.	First Hurdle Race in Japan	200
XXV.	Voyage through the Japanese Inland Seas	206
XXVI.	El Dorado	219
XXVII.	A Day in Sonora	227
XXVIII.	The Parks of America	234
XXIX.	A Hunting Misadventure	251
XXX.	Career of an Emigrant	261

LIST OF ILLUSTRATIONS.

Tropical Pall-Bearers		*Frontispiece.*
"Last Chance," *late* "Now or Never"	*to face page*	31
At Bay	,,	59
Our Camp	,,	90
Incapable of Mischief	,,	117
A Rude Intrusion	,,	153
The Patriarch's Attendants	,,	239

ALL ROUND THE WORLD.

CHAPTER I.

BOYHOOD AND MISCHIEF.

MY FATHER was a good and ardent sportsman; as a shot he was inferior to few, while I have never met any person who could beat him as a fly-fisherman; even till the last days allotted him on earth, he could find pleasure by the brawling stream, and although his eye had lost its brilliancy and his hand its quickness, still numerous were the fine trout and salmon that rewarded his labour.

Doubtless it is from my father that I inherit this enthusiasm for field sports which has induced me to seek game in almost every portion of the globe, not only for the sake of slaughter, but in order to study their habits and instincts. Nor am I satiated; the table may lose its attractions, the wine cup cease to gratify, and the majority of the amusements of youth become stale and tedious, still I crave for those innocent pleasures which man enjoys to perfection when alone with nature, away from the strife and turmoil of society, where the gun and rifle are his truest and most trustworthy friends.

The first episode in field sports I can remember was hunting water-rats, by the side of a beautiful trout-stream that flowed round the lower portion of the grounds attached to my boyhood's home. In those days I possessed a brace of terriers, which were my constant associates; they understood my voice as well as if they had been of my own race; they obeyed my orders more promptly than any Eastern slave; there existed between us a bond of affection that was indescribable, yet all-powerful. Wherever I went, they accompanied me; whether it was to fish, walk, or ride, Quiz and Gip were never far off, and at night they frequently became my bedfellows.

In the autumn, when the crops had been gathered and housed, the unfortunate rats sought seclusion and shelter among the tangled weeds and rushes that margined the stream, for the scythe of the reaper had exposed their ordinary retreats and hiding-places.

As soon as lessons were over, I and my canine pets repaired to our hunting-ground. The dogs knew well their work; every possible hiding-place was beaten; flags, burrs, or waterlilies, were thoroughly scrutinised, till at length a hole containing our game was found, or a new and strong trail discovered. A sharp quick bark would indicate the welcome news, and the fun and excitement soon became fast and furious. At length the game is driven to the water; a sudden splash, as if a stone had been rolled from the bank, tells the story, and one or both the dogs jump into the stream in pursuit, and swim to the centre, awaiting the reappearance of the foe. Over a minute elapses; all our nerves are strung to the utmost tension from excitement, when up comes the rat, possibly many yards from where his enemies await him; but their vision is sharp; the first break on the surface caused by the head of the pursued is sufficient for their quick sight, and at the unfortunate they go. A stroke more, and one might fancy the pursued would be in Quiz's clutches. Not so. Just as the dog is about to seize the prey, the crafty rodent dives, and this game is played again and again, till the poor vermin, exhausted and half drowned, fails to get below the surface with sufficient rapidity, and so loses its life.

When I was about twelve, a great event took place in my hunting career. It was at the end of autumn, and a cold, wintry sun illuminated the joyless landscape. I was returning home after a long tramp, while my companions (the dogs) trotted wearily at heel, for they had run themselves almost to a stand-still in pursuit of hares and rabbits. Suddenly they both uttered a short quick yelp and rushed from me. I followed at best speed, and just as I turned a corner of hedge, I saw a large polecat enter a dilapidated piece of wall not more than a couple of yards in front of his pursuers. Rats had been large game previously, but here was an adversary that far eclipsed them. Never had I seen the dogs so excited; they positively screamed out their rage, and even gnawed the stones that afforded a temporary sanctuary to their enemy. An hour's labour failed to dislodge the foe, and my success appeared more than doubtful, when a labourer came up and helped me to demolish the old structure of granite and mortar. Hereupon the polecat, finding the position untenable, made a sally, but he was unable to fight through his foes, and a moment later game little Gip had him by the loins, in a grip which would have killed a much larger adversary. The odour which the polecat emitted during our efforts to get at him, and after his death, did not frighten the dogs. On the contrary, ever afterwards, when such an effluvia would greet their nostrils, the hair on their backs would rise, and their eyes flash with more than ordinary excitement.

My first shooting experiences began at school in the neighbourhood of the beautiful town of Hamilton, Lanarkshire. On returning, after the holidays, one of our number related how, during his visit at home, he had fired a gun and killed the object of his aim. He dilated with such flowing language upon the pleasures of shooting, and the easiness of becoming a crack shot, that we all became smitten with an eager longing to be possessors of a gun. A collection among my schoolfellows, amounting to twelve and sixpence, was made for this purpose, and a committee of three appointed to superintend the outlay of the public funds. The starter of the idea was of course selected as one of the honourable trio, for he had become a great man, in the estimation of his fellows, since his home-exploits. I also was honoured with office, because my father was a military man, and because I was destined to serve my Queen and country, and was therefore expected to know more of fire-arms and their use than the common crowd. The third—and here the sense of my countrymen was exhibited—was selected for his shrewdness in making bargains, for although he never spent any money or brought playthings from home, yet always before the term was over his stock of tops, marbles, bats, and balls exceeded all others. What he was in boyhood, he is now in mature years—a wealthy but still hard-working successful foreign merchant.

Having secretly made enquiries, one Saturday afternoon we sallied forth to visit a tinkering gunsmith. Long and serious was our conference ; at length a bargain was struck—I might rather say that we obtained three bargains ; namely, an old and dilapidated gun-stock, the lock of an antiquated horse-pistol, and a barrel, red with rust, but declared to be of most superior quality. The smith undertook to put these together, and have them ready for use that day week.

The intermediate time passed slowly. Friday had arrived, when a most serious and previously unforeseen difficulty arose. Who was to go for the gun ? All shirked this responsible duty; to carry fire-arms, even through back streets, in broad daylight was more than any one dared. First one was saddled with the task, then another, each in his turn being accused of cowardice when he refused. Angry words ensued, and even a battle in which one of the combatants got a severe black eye. At length we determined to cast lots to decide who was to perform the objectionable office, and the unlucky number fell to me. School was dismissed at the usual hour on the important Saturday; my companions were to assemble in a little copse in a neighbouring orchard, where I was to join them with the gun. When I reached the gunsmith, and received our purchase, I confided my fears to its vendor. Fortunately I did so, for he truly proved a friend, and despatched his assistant with the treasure to the place of rendezvous, which I reached by a different route. With due comments, and advice from all, under the supervision of the gunsmith's boy, our single barrel was loaded. To whom was the honour of the first shot to be confided? With universal acclamation, the companion who had shot during the holidays was selected; but to our surprise he modestly declined the offer. Some went so far as to say he was a muff and afraid, and had never fired a gun in his life; but even such insinuations would not alter his determination. As the gunsmith's assistant was second choice, he took the weapon with the air of a man; his courage and manner made a great impression, and he temporarily became a hero. Next, for a victim. Each limb and bough was searched, and at length an unfortunate robin, whistling, yet shivering in the cold autumnal atmosphere, was found; the crowd halted, the adventurous marksman advanced; some dared the advice that "Now was the time! You are close enough!" What impertinence to pretend to know more of projectiles and their range than a gunmaker's assistant! Closer, closer he crept, with cautious measured stride; every beholder held his breath; not five yards severed the songster from his destroyer; the gun was raised, an aim taken, oh! such a long aim — from its length doubtless we considered it very deadly; a report followed, all rushed to the scene, and scarcely more than a bunch of feathers remained to tell the tale of the murdered robin !

Various were our successes that day ; we brought down a blackbird and thrush, while I winged a house-sparrow. Then with our game and the gun dismembered we stealthily, like guilty marauders, sought the awe-inspiring school-precincts. Shooting was, you may suppose, the sole subject of that evening's conversation. Those who had been so fortunate as to kill were heroes ; those who had missed were never tired asking for details which might ensure success.

As our gun required washing after so much work, a quiet hour, when all in the house were supposed to have retired to rest, was selected for the purpose. Portions of shirts, with innumerable pocket-handkerchiefs, were sacrificed, and voluntarily offered for this service, when, to the surprise of all, in walked the Dominie ! All fled to their couches in dismay, and our well-prized and proved gun fell into the hands of the enemy, never again to revert to its rightful owners. Not only did we suffer this loss, but on Monday all were arraigned ; the surreptitious introduction of the weapon formed the subject of a court of enquiry, and each of the supposed ringleaders got a jolly good whacking.

Months rolled by ; the punishment I had received on the occasion just stated had lost much of its effect through the lapse of time, and I was again seduced into a shooting escapade. A big boy, two years older than myself, had arranged with a cotter for the loan of a gun at the rate of sixpence for the afternoon. Funds, however, were wanted for ammunition ; and as I was known to be flush, and, at the same time, trustworthy, I was admitted into partnership. Without mishap we arrived at our hunting-ground, the margin of a brook, near which rabbits had been seen. With bunny our acquaintance did not amount to intimacy. At last a water-hen was flushed; she flew into a tree, where she was ignominiously and unfeelingly slaughtered. When our game was picked up, a horrible thought struck us. Perhaps we had been guilty of a violation of the game laws. The dead bird and gun would certainly lead to our detection, and then we should be shut up in gaol. Accordingly, we resolved to hide the gun in some grass, and sink the bird in the first deep pool we reached, by tying a stone to its feet. Our guilty conscience for many a long day caused us to bury this secret in our bosoms. In fact, for weeks after the transaction, any unusually forcible ring at the hall door caused my heart to jump into my throat, as I felt certain it must emanate from an officer of the law, clothed with powers which would justify our arrest, dead or alive.

At length school-days ended—alas, that they should! for my young friends will find, as time rolls on, that they are not the least happy of life—and from a relation I accepted, with the approval of my parents, an invitation to Cumberland. This was a delightful visit. I was actually trusted with a double-barrel, and had a pony to ride on. Which I enjoyed the most, it would be difficult to say. One portion of the day I was on horseback, the other dealing destruction to the unfortunate feathered beauties that came in my way. Now that I am older, and, I hope, wiser, I regret having been the cause of such objectless massacres.

As for the pony, I broke his knees jumping a fence large enough for a thorough-bred to tumble over, and he therefore was unfit for work till time had patched up the injury. For shooting by accident an old and valued hen belonging to a neighbouring Quakeress lady, I was deprived of fire-arms: and without gun, without horse, I became most miserable; in fact, they had become part and parcel of my existence, and the deprivation of them was the greatest punishment I could suffer.

Moping about one day, not knowing what to do, a terrier of well-known pluck followed me, for I and the dogs of all degrees were ever intimate. I entered a large grass field, in the lower portion of which a flock of geese were feeding on the margin of a horse-pond. Without thought, "Pincher" was ordered into the water, probably with the intention of intimidating the birds; but he mistook my meaning, seized the gander by the neck, the rest of the flock rushed to the rescue, and, to save the dog's life, I had to wade up to my waist to assist him. It was a splendid fight. The dog's pluck would not permit his surrendering or letting go the enemy, while the bird's comrades stuck to their chief with the most persistent courage. Doubtless but for a stick I had picked up and used with hearty good-will Pincher would have been drowned. As it was, he received numerous severe bruises; but, in return, he deprived the gander of life. However, my escapade had been seen, the story was exaggerated, and, after a lecture on the disgrace attached to such heinous conduct, I was, sorely against my will, despatched home to Scotland.

With advancing years my love for shooting and fishing increased. Cricket and foot-ball were neglected; peg-tops and marbles ceased to be attractive. I craved solely for the excitement of field sports. At length a chance occurred. A kind old uncle paid my father a visit; and on leaving, he gave me a very genuine tip, a portion of which I determined to spend in a fishing excursion to the Highlands. A description of the capture of my first salmon may not be uninteresting.

In less than an hour I reached the spot where I intended to commence operations. I was not a little disappointed to find the water still too thick; but I hoped, by using different varieties of red hackles, to pick up a few fish along the shallow edges of the rapids. My luck was not good, and by the time Old Sol had reached his greatest altitude, I began to despair of a heavy basket, and disgust at want of success had taken a strong hold of my feelings. My appetite also put in a claim for attention; so, seating myself on a boulder close to the water, I enjoyed, with no very enviable feelings, my frugal and limited meal—

"Nursing my wrath to keep it warm."

Having thus dawdled away a couple of hours, the decline of the sun warned me that I had still some way to walk. Picking up my rod and landing-net to put my intentions in operation, I was surprised by the splash of a heavy fish not twenty yards below me, in the clear water formed by the entrance of a mountain rivulet, which, from its lesser size, had settled sooner than the larger stream. It struck me, not having seen the disturber, that it probably was a large brook trout, or, perhaps, a sea one — more likely the former — as the season had not yet arrived for these active and silvery beauties to migrate from their salt-water abodes. With bent back, and cautious, steady step, I advanced within casting distance. My heart beat faster, and all my knowledge was put in practice to throw a light and skilful fly. My father was a fisherman. What a triumph, if I should kill a larger fish than he had! With what pride should I display my prize, and afterwards narrate my prowess! Moreover, would I longer be considered a boy? Should I not have a right to claim a position among acknowledged anglers? Such thoughts as these passed through my brain rapid as electricity. How anxiously did I pray for success! What advantage would I not have taken, if opportunity offered, to become the possessor of so noble a prize! I even fear I might have been guilty of murder, and used a gaff or fish-spear to accomplish my object, if those implements had been within reach, and I could have advantageously wielded them!

My trail fly had scarcely touched the water when a dull sullen plunge was made at it, and the dark broad back of a well-grown salmon showed itself. Instinctively with the splash I struck, and with delight felt that I was fast in a foe whose claims to supremacy among the piscatorial tribe have never been disputed. The fish appeared scarcely to be aware of the dangerous game he was playing, as for some minutes it remained stationary, and one might have been doubtful of having him on but for the tremulous motion that passed up the line and rod to my hand. For several minutes the salmon remained *in statu quo*, but on my putting on a little additional pressure, my eyes were quickly opened, for with the speed of a racehorse making a Chiffney finish or the descent of a wild duck to its feeding-ground in a gale of wind, the salmon started down stream. I had but a hundred and forty feet of line on my reel, and unless I followed, I felt certain he would soon run it out and smash everything. After the foe, down river, I started, flying, running, and jumping, over stones, gullies, and rocks, which, under ordinary circumstances, I would have thought and looked at a a second time before facing. In this manner at least two hundred and fifty yards of the roughest ground was passed at a quicker pace than I have ever been able to accomplish before or since. This spurt had evidently tired the fish, although, if he could only have known how much worse was my state, he would have kept up the steam a little longer, as half a dozen strides would have fairly pumped me. But *fortuna favet fortibus*. The fish now changed his tactics, slackening his pace to a four-mile-to-the-hour pace, keeping down deeper than previously. The opportunity was not lost to reel up all line I dared take in, and to get myself in preparation and breathing condition for the next heat. One thing which makes salmon more difficult to handle than all other fish is the uncertainty of its movements; you lose one through some new stratagem, and you make up your mind to be prepared to counteract it, when the next opportunity offers, but what is your surprise when directly the opposite are the dodges followed, so that by avoiding Scylla you run into Charybdis. A salmon is also a fish of very enlarged ideas. He appears to have a perfect disregard of distance; and when he makes a start, if not stopped, he leaves the impression that he is off to the other side of the ocean or the Antipodes. My fish continued now sailing up and down, within fifteen or twenty yards, and keeping close to the bottom; an insane idea struck me of having a good look at my beauty, and I put pressure on my rod (a very light, twelve-foot trout one), but without the slightest effect. His weight was such, combined with his strength, that my tackle must have broken had I persisted. In moving along the precipitous bank my foot displaced a stone, which rolled into the river with a splash. The hint was evidently all that was wanted, and off my friend again went, with all his previous celerity; but this run was not quite as long, and, as a little alteration in the programme, the fish finished the burst by jumping three times out of the water, giving me a good opportunity of judging his weight and proportions; and previous experience told me, from his contour, that it would well turn fifteen pounds. The two heats had done their work, or his lordship was in a more amiable state of mind, as, with care, I could now stop his course and keep him closer to the surface; but an occasional angry dash of his tail warned me not to attempt too many liberties. I kept my eyes on the alert for a piece of gravel-bank on which to coax him from his element, having dropped my landing-net in the excitement of the first race because it was too small; but this was rather precipitate, for not more than half my work was over. Up and down I walked, gave line and took it in as opportunity offered, and I began to think that I was more of a victim than my *attaché*. Over forty minutes had I been playing my fish and taking the most violent exercise, undergoing at the same time the greatest mental excitement, and yet I was apparently as far from success as at the start. The only part of the river I could find where the bank sufficiently shelved to slide him ashore was on the other side, so across I went. These mountain brooks are treacherous things to wade; from six inches of water, the next step you take may be to your neck, if not farther; and if, when so agreeably situated, the enemy should take another fancy, and challenge you to a third heat, good-bye to all your hopes—your castles in the air would most ruthlessly be demolished. After getting in up to my waist, I safely landed without accident, and, after one or two unsuccessful attempts, got my prey into shoal water, out of which, with a dexterous hoist with both hands, I transferred my victim to *terra firma*. My fatigue, exertion, and wetting were now all forgotten, and I fairly yelled with pleasure. Again and again I looked at him, and never tired admiring his gigantic and handsomely developed proportions. Many and many a time have I recalled that day, and remember with greater pleasure the killing of my first salmon than almost any sporting adventure in an adventurous life.

Next year, with my parents, I removed to Ireland. Our residence was in the centre of a good hunting, shooting, and fishing county; and as my education was supposed to be completed, I had nothing to do but enjoy myself. Those were happy days. I can never forget them. With what pleasure did I exhibit to my dear old father the results of my exertions and skill! how delighted did I feel on receiving his commendation! And then, when my beloved mother would express uneasiness lest I should over-fatigue myself or catch cold, I would cast my arms around her, and kiss away all her alarms. Take my advice, young gentlemen: value and respect your parents while they are with you; attend to their admonitions, for when it is the will of Providence to remove them, their place can never be refilled. Their solicitude is the result of pure unselfish affection, such as you will never find in the cold, pitiless, unfeeling world.

But time fled on rapidly. I became fretful and unsettled; a desire to roam had taken possession of me; no longer had small game the same attraction. At night, in my dreams, tigers and bears howled around me; at one moment, I had a hairbreadth escape; next I shot single-handed the dreaded man-eater, till I became so discontented and uneasy that I shunned society, and kept entirely to myself.

CHAPTER II.

MY FIRST STEEPLECHASE.

ABOUT this date I got into a sad scrape. A thoroughbred mare, which my father had possessed and ridden as his charger for many years, was the dam of a four-year-old colt, very handsome and valuable. This colt was the old gentleman's pet. Every day he visited it in the stable, and seldom without taking it a piece of bread or sugar. Several times I had been permitted to cross this horse, and once ride him with hounds. I soon found out that he was remarkably fast, and a very clever fencer.

In our neighbourhood there lived a young fellow, a few years over my age, half gentleman, half jockey. As he was known to be a gambler, and not over-scrupulous in horse-flesh transactions, his character was not highly esteemed. With uneasiness my parents saw us often together, and I was repeatedly warned, though in vain, that such society would do me injury.

Returning on my pony one morning from the post

town, I met the forbidden associate. He had been schooling a slashing-looking, big, raw-boned chesnut, and spoke enthusiastically of its performances. As a belt of good galloping grass-land stretched along the road, I asked him to show me how his new acquisition moved, upon which he gave the nag his head, and shook him into a three-quarter gallop. After traversing two or three hundred yards, he ran his mount at a wall at the end of the enclosure four feet high, or possibly more. The chesnut topped it cleverly, to the delight of his rider.

"Wouldn't you like such a flyer in your stables?" said he; "he can beat any horse in the county, either on the flat or across country."

Now, although there was no denying the excellence of the horse in question, I felt perfectly certain that my father's favourite, Sir Charles, with anything like proper allowance of weight for age, could run away from such an antagonist. Nor did I hesitate to say so, which resulted in a challenge. At first I declined, knowing that my father would not let me have Sir Charles for such a purpose; but being unmercifully chaffed, up to the verge of insult, I accepted the proposal.

The amount of the stakes was a mere trifle, at the same time as large a sum as my small purse would allow, and, upon being pressed over and over again to double the bets, I was obliged to confess with shame to my antagonist that I had no more money.

That evening we met at a farmhouse, and arranged the distance, place, and date of the race. We selected the day on which my father was in the habit of going to a neighbouring city to draw his pay. Before the event came off, I succeeded in obtaining permission, through my mother's intercession, to take Sir Charles out, and each time I did so you may be sure he got a good breather. As it would not do to take the colt home warm, I arranged that a stable *attaché* should meet me some distance off, where a scrape and rub down could be given without attracting attention ; and also that the horse might come home not looking the worse for his exercise. As time passed, and the eventful date approached, more and more I wished to back out, even if I had to pay forfeit of all the stakes; but a false pride intervened. I would not listen to the small warning voice of conscience, and therefore continued to act a part towards those who loved me of which I ought to have been heartily ashamed.

With nervous anxiety, I saw my father depart on his quarterly errand. An hour afterwards, and only a few minutes before the colt should have received his noonday feed, I threw my leg over him, and started for the place of rendezvous. On reaching it I found, to my surprise, quite a number of labourers and servants assembled. The proceedings, which I hoped would not be known by any but ourselves, had leaked out ; in fact, I found that my adversary had been making a book on the results, and consequently all who had thus obtained a monied interest were naturally anxious to be spectators.

The chesnut stripped admirably, possibly a little low in flesh ; still he was much improved. The knocks and bangs he had shown on my first seeing him, and which gave him rather a stale look, had all disappeared. My expectation of winning was therefore much shaken, and but for the spectators I should have backed out; for I feared that, if I won, it would be after a hard struggle, and the colt was not in condition to endure a severe contest.

On all sides I heard the odds freely given in favour of my adversary, with but few takers. At length, when a blustering fellow, whom I knew by eyesight—he was a cattle-dealer—offered four to one against Sir Charles, and some time was passed without an acceptor, I was almost on the point of booking it myself, when a quiet inoffensive-looking man took up the offer, and entered it; at the same time observing that, sooner than disappoint any one, he would not decline repeating the operation. This revived my courage.

Just as the race was about to be run, I was joined by the silent personage, who apologised for interrupting me, and then gave me the following instructions:—"Young gentleman, I'm an old hand, know a deal more than I look to, know that chesnut since he was a yearling, know his failings and his good points, for I have often had a leg over him. Just take my advice: make a waiting race of it. Let him lead you till the last jump is over; and then, if you can't beat him in the straight run home at the finish, the fault is yours, not your horse's. There's a stun in your favour; and big as the other looks, he never could carry weight; them that's tallest on their pins hain't always the most substance."

Never being above listening to advice, but using my own judgment whether to act upon it or not, I saw at once that the unknown speaker was correct in his idea of how the race should be ridden, and no person, fortunately, had overheard his instructions.

After a glance at the girths, I quietly gained my saddle, and joined my adversary, who was impatiently waiting my arrival, for his mount was extremely fidgety. Without difficulty we got away, the chesnut forcing the running, and hauling his rider nearly out of his seat. I followed without pushing, and, ere a quarter of a mile was passed, found, to my great relief, that my foe was far inferior in speed, provided he was now really going his best.

None of the fences exceeded the average of hunting-jumps, excepting the last, which was a post and rails, with water on the landing-side. This leap, although stiffish, was only awkward from a drop in the ground where you came at it; and from previous experience of Sir Charles's capacities, I had little dread but that he would be able and willing to take me safely over.

Up to this time scarcely four strides had separated us. Evidently it had been the object of my opponent to force the pace. As we approached the last fence, he found out that such a game was impossible, so adopted a new stratagem, which is often successful when a young horse is the opponent. He rushed his horse at the last fence, and caused the animal to baulk, just as he gathered his legs under him to make the leap. But I was too close abreast of him for the ruse to succeed. With a touch of spur and whip, as well as a word of encouragement, Sir Charles, without falter, rose to his leap, and, as the saying goes, took me halfway into the next field ere he touched ground again. My adversary knew that he was beaten; he never attempted to make up lost distance; so I cantered past the winning-post an easy conqueror.

Boy-like, and even man-like, I felt no small amount

of pleasure at the result, though my conscience warned me that my father would be excessively annoyed, when the story reached his ears. Had I possessed courage to endure the chaff about being still in the nursery which was showered down upon me, I should not have been in my present difficulty.

I got my horse home without exciting suspicion. Even the old groom made no remarks on his appearance, for, previous to returning, behind a hay-rick Sir Charles had undergone a good grooming from two ablebodied stable-lads; nor had he suffered in heart, for never did I feel the brave colt travel homewards more cockily. Still I was uneasy, and again and again during the few hours preceding my father's return I visited his stall. Fortunately he continued all right. He emptied his manger with more than usual appetite; and I was thankful to find that, although I had been disobedient and deceitful, I had not done the animal injury.

At length the old gentleman returned. A dark frown was settled upon his face, and when he told me in a peremptory manner that he wished to see me in his room, I knew the secret was out. I will pass over what happened, except to say that my father perceived that travelling was the best remedy for my restless, adventurous spirit, and gave me permission to go abroad.

By this time I had become a proficient in the use of the gun and rod. I had already killed almost every description of British game, as well as sundry salmon. I also had learned to tie either a trout or salmon fly equal in finish to those emanating from the hands of a professional. Hitherto I had shot for the sake of boasting of the numbers I could bag; but a change, possibly resulting from my skill, took place. The habits of game and their modes of life became my constant study. To see my setters hunt and display their sagacity was enjoyed; to see the game go off scathless, although in my power, was a still greater pleasure.

Since then I have ceased to shoot when my bag has been sufficiently replenished, and my forbearance has produced a higher feeling of satisfaction than I should have otherwise enjoyed.

I am glad to say that the class of naturalist sportsmen is rapidly increasing—men who shoot for the sake of the exercise and pleasure it produces, who are satisfied with a moderate remuneration; so different from those who crave for wholesale slaughter, and feel only gratification in having brought to bag every unfortunate that was flushed before them. All who shoot are not really sportsmen; many of them should rather be called butchers.

It is the same with horsemanship. If emergency cause it, such as sickness or imperative and undelayable business, it is excusable to ride a horse till he suffer from extreme fatigue; but if such an ordeal is demanded simply to gratify whim, caprice, or pleasure, it is an offence that should be unpardonable in the eyes of all proper-thinking persons.

A very short period before going abroad, I killed my first deer. It was thus: the park wall of a neighbouring nobleman's demesne, for upwards of a hundred yards, had been blown down; half a dozen deer had in consequence escaped, which, one by one, in detail had been killed, with the exception of an old buck, who eluded all pursuit. Shooting rabbits one evening, I observed his track in the margin of a field of young wheat. On a further examination, I found several "forms" where he had lain, while the farmer who owned the crop informed me that he had seen the buck on numerous occasions, and, further, expressed a desire that some one would shoot him, as he was doing much damage. For several evenings at sunset I took a stand, in each instance guided by the wind, as I learned the marauder always entered at the same spot. However, for over a week I was unsuccessful. Being foiled so often, I had almost determined to give up the chase; but an acquaintance of my family, who had paid us a visit, begged of me to make one more effort, and let him be my companion.

Half an hour before the sun went down, we reached our hunting-ground, and disposed ourselves behind a portion of a fence, which offered such shelter as would screen us from observation.

Long and anxiously we lay *perdus*, and were about to retire, disgusted at our want of success, when to our delight the object of our visit made his appearance. The light was gradually waning, and with anxiety we watched his slow and guarded approach to the ambuscade. My companion was to shoot first; at length I gave him the signal to do so, and following the report, the buck sprung into the air, and at a slashing gallop made for a neighbouring wood. I pitched my rifle and took a steady aim; the shot was a long one, still the bullet told, for again the deer showed indications of being hit, by almost coming on his knees, and, with difficulty recovering himself, afterwards departing at accelerated pace for parts unknown. Next day the buck was found dead, nearly a couple of miles off—the first shot had grazed him in front of the shoulder, the second had hit him in an excellent line, but with rather too much elevation to kill him on the spot.

Before leaving home and those ties so delightful to be remembered, I will add another adventure. I was stationed with my regiment at Fermoy, in County Cork, and as it was the summer season, and the fishing was excellent, whenever I was off duty, I was in the habit of spending a large portion of my time on the edge of the river Bride. With many years' experience and frequent visits to the most celebrated fishing-streams, I have never, in the course of my life, met with a rivulet so admirably adapted for the use of the fly as that picturesque and beautiful tributary of the Blackwater. In addition to the water being as clear as crystal, it flows through as rich a valley of cultivated land as it would be possible to find; the margin is almost entirely clear from obstructions, thus affording ample space to cast a long line. During the heat of the day I had not been blessed with much success, and as I was aware that towards sunset the fish would be on the feed, and that probably I should be able to make up any deficiency, I resolved to remain. The village of Rathcormack was near, so I dismembered my rod and took possession of the well-sanded parlour of the hotel, ordering the ubiquitous waiter to furnish me with the standing dish of those parts, rashers and eggs, with which to allay my increasing appetite. I have always had a love for eating a meal in one of those neat wayside taverns, with their white-sanded floors. However simple it might be, whatever you partake of is so plain, yet appetising, that after the luxury of mess-dinners the contrast is a relief. As the sun approached the horizon, I restarted to try my luck, and soon had reason to congratulate myself on the result. The fish were fairly ravenous, and although they did not run large, I rapidly filled my creel with those of the proper size to be most acceptable at the breakfast-table. I fished two pools with the above success, and had moved down to the third, where, from its being deeper and less-frequented, I had little doubt I should even do better. The first few casts assured me that my suppositions were correct, and many a handsome brilliant-hued trout was added to my already plenteous store. Down the stream I travelled till I stood upon a gravel-bank where the water was contracted and more rapid. Several more fish were captured, and as the light had become dubious, I had made up my mind to stop further proceedings. In taking a few farewell casts, I observed something swimming on the surface which at first I took to be a dog; but on closer examination the physiognomy was so totally different from any canine I had ever seen that I was forced to conclude that I was mistaken. What could it be? I turned the question round in my mind, and at last came to the conclusion that it was nothing more or less than an otter. These amphibii, I was aware, were well known all along the lovely valley of the Blackwater, and more particularly in the vicinity of the picturesque grounds of Castle Hyde, and my present apparition, without doubt, had come from these haunts, deservedly lauded for their beauty. The animal, apparently, did not perceive me, so actively was he employed on his own private affairs. Several times he dived and as rapidly rose to the surface, stemming the rapid current with an ease and dexterity far excelling any terrestrial animal of my acquaintance. From the moment of noticing the stranger, I had stood motionless, and by degrees he had steadily advanced till just abreast of my position, and not over forty feet from me. A strange idea struck me: why not throw my flies over him, and with a quick strike stick a hook in his glossy well-clad hide? Acting on the spur of the moment, I made my cast, and, with the first effort, had a contestant fast at the end of my line, a thousand times more troublesome than ever I had before or since. By paying out line at one moment, next minute gently taking it in, and always retaining a steady strain, the despoiler of hundreds of the finny tribe, though making every effort that he thought would avail him in such an emergency, could not free himself from the insidious barb. My line was strong, but my rod light and very pliable; so I discarded the latter, and having run out through the rings the greater portion of what my reel contained, I played the adversary as if with a hand-line. Flesh and blood could not stand the issue further, and at length, by wading nearly up to my knees, I succeeded in getting my antagonist into the landing-net, which fortunately was an unusually large, strong, and deep one. So far, I had succeeded admirably, but how to retain my prisoner and keep him a captive, I knew not. His formidable molars, when he had time to think a bit, would soon free him; and keep my prize, if possible, I was determined on. A thought struck me. If I could only get his tail, which hung over the edge of the landing-net, into the sleeve of my coat, and tie it tightly round with a string, his flight would be so impeded that, with a fair open country for our run, I had little doubt but that I would be the fleeter of the two, the other having a very awkward, although not heavy, handicap. Without delay, I attempted the process, and never in the course of my life had I as hard a game. Still, I stuck to it, and what with putting my foot on his neck and trying to hold him on the ground, breaking my rod and getting the slack of the line round my feet, so as to hamper me almost inextricably, I at length secured my prey. With much difficulty, and several nearly successful attempts at escape, I gained the village, when I snugly put my captive in the well of an Irish car, and brought him home in triumph.

On close inspection, I found that I had only a kitten, or, in other words, a half-grown otter to deal with. Save me from thus tackling one of them that had attained maturity, if their strength and unconquerable determination increases in due ratio with their stature! For some days the brute was sulky and untouchable, but, within a week, he had formed a great attachment for a Skye terrier which I possessed, and in a month from the date of capture became so reconciled to his new home and master that he would follow me wherever I went, provided the dog was one of the party. For months I kept him, and he would bask with delight in front of a good fire, with a gusto that was indisputable; and quite a good understanding had sprung up between us, when, unfortunately, he strayed out into the barrack-yard without a protector, and was pounced upon by a savage greyhound, who rapidly enlisted confederates among the useless curs that were near, and after making a gallant fight, the stranger had to surrender, gamely struggling to the last against superior numbers.

CHAPTER III.

A RUN WITH THE GIBRALTAR FOXHOUNDS.

WITH home I have now done. Let us proceed to a more sunny land; one teeming with romance and poetry, a land where British blood has often been shed, and British honour often vindicated. Let us repair to Spain, and halt at that famous fortress, which guards the entrance to the deep blue Mediterranean Sea. Many a delightful day have I passed on that renowned rock, where the proud British ensign waves within sight of the swarthy Spanish soldiery; and many a pleasant adventure have I met with in the picturesque country adjoining the Anglo-Saxon settlement. Gibraltar, familiarly Gib, although a rock, and of no great proportions, is a most jolly quarter: here an officer's duties are heavy, but the amusements plentiful. Balls, pic-nics, riding and boating parties are in the cool weather in such abundance that vacant time seldom hangs heavily on your hands. And then those walks along the Almada after mess! Who can forget the saunters there? Such picturesque costumes, pretty senoritas, bright pairs of eyes—such feet and ankles—such walking Venuses, as only are to be seen among Andalusian belles! We are all mortal, and the impressions of youth are not easily effaced. But we will pass over the fair sex, and, instead of the brunette beauties, treat of the spotted ones that form the pack well known to every military man as the Calpe Foxhounds.

To the noble house of Beaufort, I believe, the Gibraltar garrison are indebted for establishing this hunt. For years drafts from their home-establishment have annually been forwarded as a gift to make up casualties, for, strange to say, hounds bred at the Rock are deficient in scent; so our readers will see that, if the Calpe hounds do not kill whenever they meet, the pack is at least composed of material inferior to none in England. In the month of February, 18—, the powers that then had control of the kennels determined that the next meet should take place at the second tower, Eastern Beach. This is the best riding and safest find in the country; so it is no wonder that a large field always assembles on such occasions. Even those of the fair sex who were equestrians turned out in force to see the throw off, and perchance have a mile-or-two breather, within sight, or at least sound, of the melodious beauties. Previous to the day of which I speak, there had been a great deal of friendly competition in the hunting-field between the officers of two regiments that had served shoulder to shoulder in Russia and afterwards in the distant East. Even the privates of these corps, I think, never had a squabble; but on the occasion in question it was to be decided who possessed the best horsemen or the best mounted man; the individuals, therefore, who took upon

"LAST CHANCE," *LATE*, "NOW OR NEVER."

their shoulders the responsibility of representatives were doubtless determined to do their utmost to win the laurels.

The day broke dry and cloudy. A shower during the night had made the soil springy, perhaps a trifle heavy, but otherwise all foretold a hunting morning rare to be found, and the knot of top-boots that assembled in the mess-room to breakfast congratulated each other on the prospect; interlarding it with no small amount of chaff as to where various persons would be at the finish of the coming run.

I possessed a bay stallion at that time, fast and lasting. In the severest runs previously obtained he had proved himself gifted with extraordinary bottom, but a more thorough fiend never was girthed, for both teeth and heels he was equally expert with and equally prone to make use of. To him fell the honour of being selected for this occasion; so at an early hour the groom started with him for the place of rendezvous.

The ride along the Eastern Beach is dreary in the extreme for the first few miles after you pass through the Spanish lines, for a wide slope of sand extends before you, girt on one side by the Mediterranean, on the other by a chain of rugged sierras. Here and there, but far between, an occasional cabin is to be found; and if you should catch a glimpse of the swarthy residents, what between dirt and sun-burning, they look as dark, or darker, than the inmates of a home gipsy-encampment. When a small amount of ground in the vicinity of these domiciles is cultivated, the enclosure is hedged with the flowering aloe, which forms a most impenetrable fence.

In fact, at Anger, in the island of Java, this same shrub is used as a *chevaux de frise* around the Dutch earthworks that command the watering-place. The first tower, Eastern Beach, passed, the country begins gradually to improve. The mountains lose much of their rugged and sterile look; and the flat that extends between them and the sea increases into a wide grass plain, here and there dotted with brush, intersprinkled with an occasional palmetto, a good and not unfrequent cover for red-legged partridge, and a favourite haunt for quail at the periods of migration. A little farther on is a river, on the overflowed edges of which in winter I have bagged many a brace of snipe.

But we are already at the rendezvous. About thirty members and visitors are assembled, and various little parties are seen in the distance approaching to join in the anticipated run. The hat at length goes round, the master looks pleasant, the huntsman business-like. When each attendant has handed in his mite, time is pronounced to be up, and off we trot to draw a favourite and safe find. To the new arrival from home the Spanish horses look both unsightly and undersized. Still they are game and lasting, though usually slow and mulish; but they are admirably adapted to their country, for with unerring foot they will canter over ground so uneven and covered with boulders that to walk an English horse over the same would most probably result in broken knees, or even worse. This unsightly appearance in these horses is principally caused by their being frequently goose-rumped, with the tail set on unusually low, while the crest and withers of many are remarkably high.

The cover at last reached, at a wave of the master's hand the hounds break in with a rush; stumps of cigars are now thrown away, hats pressed more firmly on the head, and eligible places selected, according to the opinion of riders, for getting away with the pack when they break cover. After a few minutes a whimper is heard. "Lady's voice!" a knowing one exclaims in a suppressed whisper. However, all again is still for two or three minutes. Then two or three hounds speak, followed by the whole pack in concert, deep, sonorous, and earnest. The place is certainly too hot; pug must break. What's that? Some one shouting "tally-ho!" But, confound such luck! that Spanish shepherd and his curs have headed our game just as it was about to take the best line of country the hunt possesses. Up and down cover the beauties race; Rantipole's voice awakening the reverberating echoes from the neighbouring hills. And well may he possess such powerful lungs, for seldom was there a truer, stauncher, or more enduring hound. But such work cannot last long in a few acres, and poor Pug, in preference to again facing the open, gets chopped.

From here we took off to another spinney, better even than the first. Our master is generally a quiet man, but from the expression of his countenance now, I pity the unfortunate who again heads back our quarry. Lord Scamperdale might be more blustering, but I doubt if half so forcible. To prevent such ordeals a short halt takes place, when we all receive a caution, and again the hounds are thrown in. The ground here is somewhat irregular, but from an over-hanging brow a perfect view can be obtained. On this are soon perched old field officers, several captains of the former *régime*, and a goodly array of subs, many looking as if they had only just left school and their mothers' apron-strings. Nothing has yet occurred to thin the field, and many, I won't say of what kind, feel and express delight that they have already been present at a kill. Soon two or three of the young hounds again open, the whipcord is heard in vigorous play, for a brace of deer, instead of our legitimate quarry, steal away over the opposite brow. By the bye, what kind of deer are these? I have several times seen them, once rode almost on the top of one, and if they are not fallow deer they bear the strongest resemblance to them I ever saw. Again the skirters settle to their work, and ere long a perfect babel of voices foretells game to be on the move. A fox from here was ever known to afford good sport. The cork woods are generally the point made for, and they are not less than ten miles distant. I have just taken up another hole in my girths, and congratulated myself that the crowd of brother subs did not seduce me into a schooling match *en route* from the one cover to the other, for while their horses look warm and fretted, mine is as cool as at the moment he left the stable, and deuced glad am I of it, for the old huntsman rattles past, and calls out, "None of your horses has a leg too many for the day's work before you."

We never had a chance of heading either fox or hounds, even supposing it had been desirable; in fact, it was all the majority of us could do to get away on anything like fair terms. As we enter the lower grounds, the galloping is heavy, and heavy weights and light nags begin to drop behind. In those days I could ride ten stone; and I do not think there was a horse in the garrison of greater substance and size than my mount, save it were the imported charger of a field-officer, and if so, the owner thought too much of him to let him figure in such an escapade. My nag never appeared to feel stronger under me than on this occasion. Although boring a little, I kept him well within his stride, and, wondrous to say, he was giving his running kindly, and had dispensed with the series of buck jumps and kicks that usually formed the preliminary flourish to a gallop. After the first mile of flat valley land had been passed over, and the half-dozen jumps that intersected it, the field had wonderfully tailed off. The master, whip, a hard-riding gunner, a big sapper, and an infantry man of the corps, already referred to, were still in front. The next flight of the ruck were by my side, many of whom I already saw would not hold out for another mile. In a short time I drew away from the crowd, and soon was close by my antagonist. The four leading men made a *détour* to the right; probably from knowing the country better, and what was before them. I should have followed the example, but when about to do so, my temporary foe, the crack of the competing corps, called upon me to follow; I was close at his heels and scarce could decline the gauntlet. A brook was before us with sedgy margin, deep and sullen as a canal; at it we both went at racing pace, my friend a little in advance; and after a scramble on the off-side, for some moments doubtful whether a ducking or not was in store for me, the powerful hind-quarters of my horse carried the day and saved me a wetting. The hounds had now turned to the right; those who had gone in that direction had luck on their side, and consequently again cut in front; the ground was still soft, yet by keeping my horse well together, I felt he had plenty left in him and to spare. A couple more water-jumps and some meadows were soon got over; the whip was just in before me when his horse made a bad flounder and finished off by coming on his head. Alas! poor Calpé never rose again; it was his last run, the finish of a long and gallant career, drawing his last breath with the saddle on, following the pack he had for many years held a good place with. Of course I did not stop for the whip, he was not wanted till feeding-time, just as Leech's parson, who got into the brook, was not required until the coming Sunday; so I pushed for the front. The big sapper's weight had commenced to tell; every dig of the spur sent his horse's tail up instead of augmenting pace, and it required but little experience to see that the honours would be either to the master, gunner, or self. For a moment the hounds came to fault on the edge of a stream beside a ford. The master called on me to assist him. A cast was made when some Spaniards shouted "*el sorro*" from a neighbouring hill-side. Soon the beauties were lifted and laid on; the soil was firmer and the pace proportionably faster, heads up and tails down; the spotted pack seemed to fly, giving utterance to their feelings in short snatches of voice, which invariably foretells the end of the drama and the close proximity of poor Pug. As we advanced, the ground became rougher, loose boulders were scattered everywhere, just such as a winded horse would toe ; but luck favoured us, and all kept our feet. If the field had tailed off, so had the pack, not over four or five couple remained, who were so closely bunched that, if a sheet would not have covered them, it would nearly have done so. Every moment all expected to run into view, and just as our desire was realised, Pug, draggled and travel-stained, scarcely able to get up more locomotion than a trot, managed to draw himself into an earth.

We had all had enough ; the gunner's horse, as he dismounted, staggered, and as for the major's, I never could tell how he held his own, for the mount was undersized, and rather inclining to the weedy order ; however, for many a week afterwards the poor beast (the horse) did not show in the hunting-field. After a sufficient halt to slacken girths and breathe our horses, talk over the run, light a weed, and take a pull at our flasks, home was the word. Saint Roque was *en route ;* before reaching there, several straggling hounds had been picked up, and as we enjoyed a draught of McCray's milk punch, others joined. The day was now far spent, the sun was already dipping over the hills that back Algesiras, and if we wished to get into the garrison before gun-fire, it was time to be jogging along. What remained of the foremost leaders of the pack we had only just time to deposit at their kennel when the evening gun belched forth the warning that all who desired to sleep within the walls of Gibraltar had better not delay, for the laws against opening the gates are as positive and unchangeable as those of the Medes and Persians.

The horse that carried me that day is dead. He died in the hunting-field, where his bones, like empty champagne bottles around an Indian or other encampment, remained as a monument to speak of the generous spirit that was contained therein.

CHAPTER IV.

RAMBLES IN SPAIN.

SHOOTING generally commenced at Gibraltar in the month of October, for earlier in the year the weather was too warm to tramp over the rough and stony hill-side in search of red-legged partridge, and the flights of migratory quail then pushing for the southward had not arrived.

The partridge-shooting, however, seldom lasted over a week or two, for sportsmen are here too numerous in proportion to the quantity of game and the size of the range of accessible country; but if the visitor should find it convenient to push inland into Spain, say twenty-five or thirty miles, he will receive an ample reward for his trouble. Through the cork wood is situated a village, called Boccaleone. It stands upon the margin of the Guadiar, and is surrounded by meadows, which in their turn are encircled by hills. Indian corn is the staple production, and in the fields where it is grown I found game abundant; and each night, as I returned homewards, quail, partridge, and hares filled the bag. Still farther off, about twenty miles inland from Tarifa, is situated an immense marsh, where, besides the aforementioned, an abundance of snipe and wild fowl can be obtained.

The *padrè* of an adjacent village must not be forgotten, for he was a most genial, good-hearted soul—a *bon-vivant* and lover of field sports. During my stay I met him daily, and when duty obliged me to bid him farewell, I did so expressing the hope that he might find it convenient to visit the garrison. A month or two afterwards he did so, and became so exceedingly popular with my brother officers that his visit was protracted over a fortnight.

During the migratory seasons good quail-shooting can be obtained of a morning at Campeamento, only a couple of miles from the landport gate. But it is the old story of the early bird and the worm. The late riser would find all the game killed or driven off ere he reached the shooting-ground.

Wild boar are also to be found, but they are scarce. On one occasion we unkenneled a veteran. Several times he ran the gauntlet through the beaters, but as often was forced on foot again. A final effort for his destruction was made, the force of shooters being so disposed that every known pass was guarded. Among the disciples of the chase was a very tall and proportionably lank engineer. He was armed with a most formidable double-barrel of French manufacture, to the end of which was attached a bayonet, terrible even to look at. Ten minutes of suspense ensued. The beaters, breaking through the brush as they approach the stands, are at length heard; the game must bolt, and bolt it did, between the engineer's legs, while both his bullets deeply bedded themselves in a neighbouring tree, and the sword-bayonet was almost as much doubled as a reaping-hook, for the aspirant for sylvan honours had been thrown off his pins, obtaining a purl that doubtless he even now well remembers. The hog had broken cover just in front of him, had been unseen and unheard till almost between our friend's legs, and the apparition was so sudden and unexpected that both head and legs were lost at the same time.

The lower class of Spaniards in the neighbourhood of Gibraltar are, with few exceptions, a most disreputable crew. It is, therefore, advisable to have as little to do with them as possible. Few seasons pass over without rows occurring between them and our countrymen, and invariably in my experience the former have been the aggressors.

I remember such a *contretemps*, in which I unfortunately figured, but luckily came off scathless. We were out hunting near the first *venta;* the hounds were at fault, and while a cast was being made, I tally-hoed, Pug stealing away. The horse which I that day rode was a black stallion of most uncertain temper; an admirable fencer when he pleased, but that was seldom. Taking my nag in hand, I ran him at a bank intervening between me and where reynard passed, that I might give the hounds a lift and place them on the fresh trail. This he cleared cleverly, and away went the pack. I tried to follow, but the bad-tempered brute, although he had jumped into the enclosure, could not be induced to jump out. Whip and spur were both plied without effect; the blackguard had sulked, and ten minutes at least were required to bully him into his senses. In the meantime a Spaniard, armed with a gun, entered the field. Without explanation or question he coolly threw his gun to his shoulder and took aim at me. I tried to wheel my horse round and ride the fellow down, but being unable to manage it, had to remain a target whether I liked it or not. The gun did not go off. I believe it missed fire, for several times he took it down as if to recock it. At length my fiend of a horse thought he had enough punishment, and I was about to wheel him round and rush at the would-be assassin, when one of my comrades, seeing my position, jumped into the field and felled the Spaniard with the butt of his crop. Neither of us waited to ask any questions as to the effect the blow had produced, but followed after the tail of the hunt.

The sea-fishing at Gibraltar is very good, but this amusement does not appear to be popular there. Although I devoted much time to it, I could seldom find a companion. One great pleasure I occasionally enjoyed was a trip in the Genoese fishing-boats from Catalin Bay to a bank four or five miles off in the Mediterranean. How delightful were those calm serene evenings—how perfect the repose—while every few minutes the deep-voiced conch-shell, used by the fishermen for signalising one another, boomed over the water!

My companions on these occasions were the most thorough personification of pirates in appearance, and often in costume—just such as you could imagine, with pistols and stilettoes sticking out of every available place, telling a fellow quietly to walk the plank, and handing him a cigarette at the same time to cheer him into the next world. Then how brown were their complexions, how black their hair and eyes! and, oh! how they smelt of garlic, an addition not inappropriate! The real pirate, I believe, should always smell of oil and garlic.

On these banks the take of fish was always large; and what between pipe and sport, and an occasional snatch of a wild Spanish song, lauding the praises of the reckless *contrabandistas*, time used to fly rapidly. It was not necessary however to go so far as this bank for sport, since all along the rocks, in the bays and indentations, from Europa Point to the Neutral Ground, especially on the Mediterranean side, fish were abundant.

With strong rod and tackle, and a sardine for bait, what beauties I have captured out of the surf beating on the eastern shore! For this work your sinker must be heavy, and the angler prepared to lose plenty of tackle, for the under-tow is very strong, the bottom rough, and the fish sometimes monsters.

In fine clear weather, when the sea is calm, trimmer-fishing afforded me much pleasure. I would set six or eight of these in a row to drift with the current, and watch them from my boat; nor would they be long left alone. Presently one would dip two or three times, then go down altogether. Hereupon, laying heartily to the oars, we would start in pursuit. Up again would come the cork, to go down and reappear in quite a different direction. To and fro we then would pursue, till a chance was afforded of using the gaff.

In the holes among the rocks eels were plentiful, and many an hour I spent in their capture. To be successful, patience rather than skill is requisite. The method was on this wise: a piece of strong cord, about eight or nine feet long, attached to a hook tied on gimp, baited with fish, was dropped into the crevices. In a few minutes, if there were any occupants, you would feel a bite. Don't be in a hurry; wait patiently, for, like a snake swallowing his food, an eel requires plenty of time. However, when you strike, do it sharply. But although we will suppose that you have now got your fish on, time will elapse before you can call him yours, for they will double round stones and squeeze themselves into all kinds of inaccessible places, from which they can only be coaxed by keeping a heavy, steady strain. The larger the fish, as may be expected, the longer will be the contest; and not unusual will be the loss of tackle, for congers have great aptitude for freeing themselves with their teeth.

Rabbits, porcupines, and red-legged partridge, abound on the upper portions of the rock, but they are strictly protected; and right it is so, for they are great ornaments to so circumscribed a space. Apes are also here to be found, but although tolerably numerous, are not often seen. In fact, many believe their existence a myth. However, two or three times I had the luck to come across them. On one occasion I was returning at break of day from visiting the sentries and guards, furnished by the detachment at Catalin Bay, of which post I was then in command. The night had been stormy and cold, with a westerly wind. The apes, which were about twenty in number, had doubtlessly come to the east side for shelter. Before the creatures saw me, I was within forty or fifty yards. Their surprise at my intrusion—their awkward attempt at escape, as they shuffled off—were very amusing.

Beside the officers' quarters at Catalin Bay there was a large mulberry-tree. The fruit, when ripe, used to disappear in the most marvellous manner. Thinking some of the men were the depredators, I lay *perdu* one bright night, with a poodle remarkable for his sagacity for my companion. At length the dog became fidgety, and rushed off, giving tongue. I followed, fortunately for the poodle, for there were at least a dozen apes, who appeared in no way intimidated till I approached. Doubtless these were the scoundrels who had deprived me of my fruit.

There are some pretty rides within access of Gibraltar. One that I frequently took and always enjoyed was to Los Varios. This village is beautifully situated in a wooded valley, surrounded by grand hills, picturesque and bold in their outline. At the *venta*, where we were in the habit of putting up our horses and having lunch, there was a true type of the Andalusian belle. She was the daughter of the host, and sometimes waited upon us. A more beautiful or graceful girl I have seldom seen. Once I met her at a bull-fight at Algesiras. Of course she was *en grande tenue* on such an occasion. Never did mantilla fall over more graceful shoulders—never did slipper cover a more beautiful foot and ankle. She did not walk—she glided over the surface of the ground, as a denizen of another world might be imagined to do.

Near Los Varios is a wild, picturesque waterfall, embedded deeply in trees and rocks. On the warmest days in summer, shade from the sun can always here be found; in the pool beneath a most delightful bath can be enjoyed. This scene has often vividly recalled some of our Scotch linns.

But I must say no more of dear old Gibraltar. How many know it, and doubtless remember the hours there passed with as much pleasure as I do!

CHAPTER V.

BARBARY FIELD SPORTS.

LONG have I gazed from Gibraltar across the Straits at the towering ranges of the irregular-outlined Atlas Mountains, that form the northern breastwork of Africa. This continent had long possessed for me the greatest attractions, and with what anxiety did I look forward to the moment when I could set foot upon its shores; for is it not the hunting-ground *par excellence* of all the world? Is it not the scene where Cornwallis Harris, Gordon Cumming, and the lion-hearted Livingstone have played their adventurous parts? True, the portion next Europe was far away from where their exploits took place; but still all was a part of the same land, undivided by impassable sea or other impediment that might prevent the migrating hordes of gnus, antelopes, and zebras, from ranging from one part to another if so disposed. Such feelings have actuated me in Scotland when wandering in boyhood in the fields in the neighbourhood of my school. The hare which sprang from its seat one moment, I hoped to see succeeded by a giant red deer, decorated with a royal head of horns, although none such were known to have their *habitat* nearer than the rocky corries of the Grampian Mountains.

But Morocco still possesses the lion, to youthful minds the grandest and noblest of all the animal creation. Not impossibly, in some of the dark shady lines caused by wooded ravines that marked the sides of the Atlas range, a royal savage, at the very moment I was gazing across, was either engaged in stalking upon his prey or making a meal on some unfortunate weaker animal.

Alas, for the days of youth and romance, of happiness and love! Value them while they last; the storm clouds that shut out the sunlight come sooner or later. And as your early years are spent, in that proportion will be the happiness of your after-life.

At length an opportunity occurred. The longed-for pleasure was to be realised. Leave of absence was obtained, and I crossed to Morocco, landing at the seaport Tangiers, which is situated upon a bay of the same name, of the area of about twenty square miles. The position of the town is picturesque in the extreme, and consists of streets built in terraces, the whole overlooked by a castle of most antiquated appearance, and flanked on either side by loop-holed masonry, that would not stand a modern bombardment five minutes. Yet this spot was once considered strong, and long protected under its guns a fleet of corsairs, who for years made navigation in the vicinity dangerous, for falling into the hands of these marine freebooters not only entailed spoliation, but probably a life of captivity. It was from a southern port of this nation that Robinson Crusoe escaped from slavery with Xury. But the glory of Morocco has fled; no ships sail under her colours, and the "Christian dog," once such an object of contempt, can now traverse the bazaars, sokes,* and mosques with perfect impunity.

The passage by steam across the Straits of Gibraltar is only a matter of two or three hours; my landing was effected with safety through a heavy surf, and the custom-house officers (who were not above accepting backshish) did not delay me unnecessarily. The hotel, after climbing through tumble-down streets, up extraordinary ascents of stairs, almost as bad as Valetta, the capital of Malta, was in due time reached, and a most comfortable as well as economic establishment it proved. Only fancy living for one dollar a-day, with table-wine included, and that within a ten-pound journey of England, and an excellent, free-to-all, unobstructed shooting-range within a few miles, with neither gamekeepers nor servants to tip! Why, to men of moderate means it appears too good to be true.

My plans were soon made through the means of an interpreter; two horses and an attendant were hired, and lunch for the following day ordered, so that when I turned in to roost nought remained but to have a good night's rest to enable me to start the campaign in Northern Africa under favourable circumstances.

Let me here give the reader a piece of advice, in case he should be tempted to visit Tangiers for the

* Market-places.

purpose of shooting. Be certain to bring your own saddlery; for however comfortably and well a Moor may ride with his knees up to his chin, I could not succeed in doing likewise, although I had had years of practice in equitation; and when from compulsion I lengthened the stirrups of this confounded invention the amount of pelt that I lost from chafing was anything but conducive to walking with pleasure after a pair of pointers, and I believe my countrymen generally are constructed on pretty much the same model as myself and have learned to ride after the same fashion. The horse of your attendant should, instead of a saddle, have only a pad, over which is slung a brace of panniers; in one of these your lunch and game can be carried, in the other your dogs. It's all very well to let a dog run ten miles from a shooting-ground when his services are not required more than half a dozen times in a season, but if you are going to use him daily or even three times a week and you are a keen sportsman, one that does not shirk walking, take my word for it, you cannot husband the strength of your canine assistants too much. It only requires thought to see that I am correct. The man who will not think of his animals' comfort, does not deserve to possess them.

Sunrise saw my *cortége* in marching order waiting at the gates of Tangiers ready to make an exit as soon as the custodian of the keys thought proper to open the barriers which cut the residents off from the surrounding country, for every night the gates are closed at sunset, and the laws against their being re-opened are as unchangeable as those of the Medes and Persians. Take warning, therefore, and do not be late, for, if such be the case, you will have to remain outside. On passing into the country, the ground is undulating and well planted, graveyards and gardens being the principal features ; a couple of miles transit through green lanes hedged with aloes discloses an open rolling landscape with distant hills and a meandering watercourse, the former clothed, the latter fringed with trees. In front and to the right, as you proceed onwards, are situated on elevated bare ground three quaint square buildings, with a large dome on the top of each ; these I was informed are the tombs of three celebrated Moorish warriors, who perished during the wars that were undertaken about two centuries back to drive the British from Tangiers, a portion of the dower of one of our queens. In the gardens woodcock, snipe, and rabbits are occasionally abundant, but as the owners of these fruitful enclosures have a strong objection to trespassers it is better to pass on and leave them undisturbed. Five miles from town, going south-west, after passing a large olive grove which grows luxuriantly at the base of a densely-wooded hill, still the haunt of numerous wild boar, extends an immense meadow through which flows a sluggish stream. On this meadow I commenced work. Snipe I found abundant, also plover. Several wild duck I flushed from the rivulet, and was fortunate enough to obtain a brace and a half of the broadbills. On leaving the damp land and ascending to more dry localities a variety of palmetto does duty for underbrush ; in this cover my dogs found several coveys of red-legged partridge, which, contrary to the nature of this species in England, lay remarkably well. As might be expected, I thinned their ranks, and also added to the weight of my now distended game-bag by the addition of a brace of bouncing hares.

Having a strong objection to be turned into a pack-horse, and knowing that if I wished to shoot well I ought to husband my strength, I handed over the results of my labour to my attendant Moor. A mile or two farther on I came to a considerable river, quite sixty yards wide, which enters the sea through a broad belt of sand—close to the grand old bluff headland, Cape Spartel. What between shooting and the allotted time for lunch and baccy, the day had fled rapidly, and although the sun was still two hours' high it behoved me to return, as the distance was eight or more miles, and I had made no preparations for remaining from home.

On another occasion, in company with two brother officers, we started in the morning, determined not to shoot till the river last mentioned was reached. On arrival there, each took a stand among the brush that grew on the margin. Our Moorish attendants we despatched with instructions to move up and down the stream and alarm all ducks they saw, well knowing the habit of these birds to follow as far as possible the water-courses on which they feed. In less than an hour we had over a dozen shots. After tiffin we beat the neighbouring open land and brush for red-legged partridge, and fortune smiled upon our labours. So at night when we betook ourselves to the Arab douar where we had arranged to sleep we produced quite a formidable array of game.

But can I ever forget that night ? I think not. After indulging in a most hearty meal—kuskasoo, a most wholesome and pleasant native dish, forming no inconsiderable portion of it,—and having imbibed a "nightcap," wearied with our day's exercise, all turned in, with the confidence of obtaining a good night's rest. Never was Somnus so devotedly courted as by your humble servant; still sleep I could not; therefore restlessly I tossed about. I was perfectly ignorant of the cause of this inquietude, and, not wishing to disturb my comrades, for a long period submitted to martyrdom. At length flesh and blood could stand it no longer; up I jumped, and sprang for the matchbox. Even the necessary time for the lucifer to become thoroughly ignited was thought a needless delay. But I found I was not the only one awake; both my friends were sitting up, and inquired almost in the same words, and at the same moment, if I also felt queer and unable to sleep, for turn which way they would, twist themselves in whatever shape they chose, slumber they could not. Scratching then became the order of the day; all had a good scratch, then halted and recommenced exercising our nails—halting more from lack of elbow-grease than from a desire to cease the operation.

But what was the cause of this itchiness? Fleas in hundreds, fleas in thousands, fleas in millions. Inside our clothes, outside our clothes, their phalanxes were equally numerous; before the lights had been put out not one had been seen, with darkness the cowardly scoundrels had stolen upon us, and that with an appetite that appeared insatiable.

With one consent we all undressed, shook our garments, brushed them, picked them over, and re-donned them, tying our drawers, waistband, and collars so tight as almost to cause strangulation, and impede the circulation of the blood. But this strategy was unavailing, the pests would not be denied admission, so all determined to make a night of it. Outside the jackals howled, inside we puffed our pipes, and occasionally moistened our damp throats, till, with pleasure, but in a very unfit state for shooting, we welcomed the entrance of our guide about an hour before daybreak.

After a hasty meal we all mounted, riding double, and started for a place known by the name of the Laguna, where we were informed wild duck were abundant. As we slowly went onward through the darkness, the ground on every side was sprinkled with glowworms, and an occasional jackal would howl a welcome of defiance. Ere the sun had risen we reached our shooting-ground; the water in the middle of the lagoon, which was free from weeds, was covered with numerous varieties of aquatic fowls. In the reeds along the margin they were almost as abundant, and for a couple of hours a heavy and successful fusilade was kept up. At length the birds became alarmed and more wary, so further work was desisted from.

While at breakfast, one of our attendants took his gun, and soon returned with a number of duck and coots. When accompanying the same man in the afternoon, I found out the cause of his success; dropping off his bournouse, the only garment which prevented him from being clothed like Adam, minus the fig-leaf, he waded into the weeds till nought but head and shoulders were visible. In this manner, with a green bough held before him for a screen, he advanced within easy range of the unsuspicious game.

On the margin of this swamp were abundant indications that it was a favourite haunt of wild boar; the marks of their wallowings were everywhere discernible, and some of the foot-prints clearly told that they had been made by giant veterans. Observing one of my dogs most uncomfortable, and bleeding about the muzzle, on examination I found a leech had fastened in the interior of his mouth, close to the root of his tongue. Leeches are here very abundant, and it is no unusual occurrence for both horses and dogs to suffer from their attentions.

With a heavy load of game we returned to Tangiers by a different route from that by which we had come. One portion of the road was very pretty, being covered with dwarf timber, among which (much improving and imparting an Eastern tone to the picture) were feeding a large drove of camels and their young. Thoroughly fatigued, we reached the gates of the city just in time to gain admission.

While in this portion of Northern Africa I had several days' hog-shooting. The haunts of these animals during the day are the rough sides of hills, in ravines and nullahs, where the brush is dense, consequently there is seldom a possibility of riding to them, and the use of the gun instead of the spear becomes admissible. Hardly any animal is gifted with more vitality, and will carry off more lead; I remember a veteran boar running the gauntlet of four double guns within easy range, and each shot told, yet the hero went off as if nothing had occurred; that evening, however, he was found dead two miles from where he received his death-wounds. At night these animals quit their lairs, and descend to the low grounds to wallow and feed on the fruits in the gardens and crops in the enclosures of the natives. From being so thoroughly nocturnal in their habits they are seldom seen, but the results of their forays are to be met with in every direction.

The general mode of shooting them is to drive the covers with beaters while the sportsmen stand on the runs, which are usually dry water-courses. As the cover is very dense, the gun should be kept at full cock, for a momentary clatter among the stones is all the warning received, and if your fire is not rapidly delivered the brute is through between your legs (very possibly knocking you over) and out of sight in a moment.

There is little or no danger on such occasions; but when the boar is wounded and brought to bay, look out for squalls if you approach him!

To the westward of Tangiers many of the consuls have fine gardens situated close to the sea. The rocks beneath are particularly grand, lofty, and rugged in their outline. Among these cliffs are numerous caves haunted by large flocks of rock-pigeons. As these birds return from their feeding-grounds just before sunset, good sport can be obtained at them. However, there is one objection to this pastime: you will find it impossible to recover nearly half the pigeons killed.

Nowhere have I seen the eagles more numerous than along this coast during the spring and autumn of the year. At these periods they are doubtlessly migrating to and from Europe. Hawks of nearly every variety are also abundant, even those of the most choice breeds.

Although I was not successful in shooting any specimens of the bustard proper (*Otis tarda*), during some parts of the year they are to be found in this neighbourhood in considerable numbers, increasing in abundance, I was informed, as you proceeded inland. The little bustard (*O. tetrax*) is, however, plentiful, and I had the pleasure of bagging many; their flight much resembles that of the curlew, and though perhaps deserving the appellation of a wary bird, with strategy they can be obtained. The best method I found was to walk outside my horse, describing gradually-diminishing circles till within range. On the table the little bustard will be found most palatable, and worthy of more trouble to kill than usually is accorded to game of greater magnitude. Storks are also numerous, but do not come under the sportsman's category of game, so I will say nothing further of them.

In the lower ranges of the Atlas fallow deer are found in considerable numbers; in the upper ranges a mammoth stag—at least, so I have been informed on trustworthy authority.

Not much is known of the distant interior, particularly towards the east coast, inhabited by the Reefians, a race of freebooters and pirates. It is a well-ascertained fact, however, that the lion is still to be found there. Fourteen or fifteen miles from Tangiers I was shown where the last lion known in that vicinity was killed. The spot was just suited for such an episode—an immense rock standing like an island among shrubs, with an open country covered with herds of goats and sheep stretching beyond.

I wish my young friends could hear the story of that lion's death narrated as told me, surrounded by a dusky crowd of stalwart manly figures, all dressed in bournouses, and leaning with pride, doubtless arising from conscious skill, upon their long single-barrelled guns. I like the Mussulman, it matters not whether he be Turk or Moor, there is a manliness and soldierly bearing about them, at the same time gentleness, that I have never found in others; but to the story.

"For many years our douars had been left in peace, our herds wandered far and wide without shepherds, for no protection was necessary. The wild beast had learned to dread the prowess of our young men, and had departed to a country where these were less brave, so no longer did our plains reverberate at night with the lion's roar— no longer did the lover dread to visit by night the village of his future bride, or the hunter fear to secrete himself to watch the grizzly boar that nightly desolated his melons.

"But a change took place. The mare of the father of Abdoul (pointing out one of the crowd) was missed, a suspicion of her being stolen came over the minds of all, for she was known far and wide as the gentlest, fleetest, most enduring and best bred possessed by the tribe. For some days most diligent search was made unsuccessfully, and hope had almost died out of ever hearing of her again, when she was discovered dead, fearfully

AT BAY.

p. 59.

mangled, among the woods that gird the slope of those hills.

"All skilled in the chase visited the spot, and the most experienced were convinced, from various indications, that the poor mare was the unfortunate victim of a beast of prey.

"The owner vowed by the Prophet to be revenged, and many promised him their assistance.

"The neighbourhood had almost relapsed into its habitual quiet, and the death of the mare had almost been forgotten, when the douar was alarmed at midday by the hurried entrance of some lads, who had seen a lion pull down a steer.

"All for some moments was commotion, but an unusual desire became paramount, to avenge the insult, and if possible rid themselves of so dangerous a visitor.

"With arms and dogs a large force mustered. On reaching the scene of bloodshed the cowardly marauder fled; he refused to face our bullets. But we followed, and here, on this very rock, he turned to defy us, his rage being thoroughly roused by our persevering pursuit, and as he stood above, his noble form defined against the clear sky, lashing his flanks with his tail and scorning the cowardly curs that yelped around, he looked every inch a king.

"But, with the help of Allah, he fell at the first fire, and his rich black mane long decorated the house of our chief. He was the last in this plain; may he never have a successor!"

Hoping to save time I returned to Gibraltar on board a felucca, a mistake I never again would be guilty of, for a gale of wind springing up an hour or two after departure, we were kept two days knocking about the Strait, with a most disagreeable sea running, and no place to obtain shelter from the elements but a hole of a cabin, redolent of oil and garlic. Cadiz or Tarifa might several times have been made, but the craft and crew belonged to Gibraltar, and very possibly were known to the Spanish Guarda Costa, for former smuggling peccadillos.

All things come to an end, and never was I more grateful than when I stretched my legs upon the mole of dear old Gib.

CHAPTER VI.

AFLOAT IN THE MEDITERRANEAN AND ASHORE IN NORTH AFRICA.

THE sail along the North Coast of Africa, from Gibraltar, particularly if you hug the land and are vouchsafed good weather, is delightful. Many times I have made this trip, but my first experience was by far the most pleasant, for the sea was smooth as a mill-pond all the way, and the vessel was navigated as close to the shore as was compatible with safety. With an awning spread over the quarter-deck I never quitted it day or night. The blue waters of the Mediterranean appeared transcendently beautiful and deep in colouring, whether by sun or moonlight. And the Atlas range of mountains, ever varying, ever grand, were constantly in sight. How I longed to land, and penetrate, in search of game or adventure, into the deep chasms and spreading valleys which were constantly exposed to sight!

After passing Algiers and its white houses, built tier over tier, the coast became less rugged and more green, and the promise of shooting more inviting. Near Cape

Bona, perhaps a hundred miles to the westward of it, to my great satisfaction on his coming on deck in the morning the Captain informed me that being short of fuel, he intended anchoring to collect drift wood. Soon after a favourable place was found, and never did I listen to cable going through hawsehole with greater pleasure. The bay into which our craft was run was almost land-locked, the hills that surrounded it were green as those of the Emerald Isle, and on the beach were assembled a swarthy crowd of Moors, anxiously scrutinising our movements, and all garbed in their favourite bournouse. Not one among us spoke their language; our intercourse was consequently conducted by signals, yet they understood, and fresh provisions in abundance were brought for our use. While the ship's company were busy I wandered off with my double-barrel; red-legged partridge and quail I found abundant, but, not having a dog, lost among the brush half the birds I killed. Here I saw several wild boar, but could not succeed in obtaining a shot at them. With a properly organised corps of beaters very different results might be anticipated. On ascending a rocky acclivity I came across a host of apes; the rascals looked at me in a most threatening manner, as if disposed to dispute my right to further progress. One old gentleman was particularly demonstrative, and at length I determined to give him the contents of a barrel. Not over twenty-five yards severed us, and he received a mortal wound; but never in my life did I regret so much firing a shot, the agony and death-struggle of the poor ape were so human, that I turned from the spot and my victim with feelings anything but enviable. From that day to this I have not shot one of that genus, nor do I believe I could be tempted to do so.

Here I had my first experience of turtle-catching. The process is simple, yet to become an adept requires considerable practice. In the warm weather, particularly at midday, they float on the surface, enjoying the heat of the sun, apparently asleep. With a boat you approach them, the crew ceasing to pull when sufficient headway has been obtained to bring you alongside your intended victims, while in the bow is posted a man whose duty is to make the capture. If the turtle is a small one it is seized by the back flipper and hauled on board, if a large fellow, the seizer, by a quick turn of his wrist after laying hold of the flipper, places the victim on its back, and, if necessary, obtains assistance to remove it from its watery home. The turtle of the Mediterranean, although good eating, are not to be compared with those of the West Indies, or Malay Archipelago. The harpoon is also used to take them, but this is considered by experts as a slovenly method, and only excusable when all other means fail.

Although we remained a couple of days, the wooding business turned out a failure, so under a half-head of steam we proceeded, and in due course of time, after running close by Pantaleria, an island where Sardinian convicts are imprisoned—it is far too lovely for such a purpose—we reached 'Malta.

While in this part of the Mediterranean, a rather remarkable instance of canine vindictiveness or revenge took place. Several of my companions had dogs on board. One was a French poodle whose antics and tricks made her the pet of all; another was a retriever, equally well educated; while a Skye-terrier was the third.

The attentions of the two latter to the lady poodle were very marked, and at length the demon of jealousy being aroused, sundry passages of teeth took place; the retriever, from his superior size, always worsting the terrier. At length, one day, the larger dog seized the smaller, carried him to the gangway and dropped him overboard. Several people saw this take place, but were unable to interfere from the rapidity with which the whole deed was transacted. The excitement on deck brought me from the cabin, when I beheld the poor little terrier swimming in the wake of the vessel. As there was a stiff breeze at the time the Captain was unwilling to lower a boat, and the terrier was consequently lost, very much to the grief of his owner.

In the autumn and spring of the year, along the coast of Morocco and Algeria, immense hordes of porpoises and tunny-fish pass and re-pass. By day and night they can be distinctly seen, rolling and plunging under the waist or stern of the vessel. From the dolphin striker which projects under the bowsprit, if you are able to hang on by the skin of your eyebrows—for the footing is limited—with the harpoon good sport can be obtained. But the moment you strike, and the victim becomes impaled, it must be dragged from the water without delay, or it will be certain to escape.

Close to Cape Bona, as the vessel skirted a headland, I perceived two bottle-nosed porpoises coming towards us. I went forward to the bow where my harpoon and line lay prepared, and three or four of the watch who were lounging on the forecastle laid hold of the slack and waited for the blow to be delivered. Soon the game was within reach, over and over they rolled, almost permitting the cutwater to bump them; at length a chance was offered and I drove the steel home. "Haul!" I shouted to my assistants, and haul they did; but the foe was too heavy, all their straining and efforts could not get the brute from the water; long was the struggle and, alas! the rope broke, when Mr. Porpoise departed at express speed, taking, as a memento of his escape, my good and well-tried harpoon.

From Cape Bon to Pantaleria is only a few hours, from the latter to Gozo about the same distance. When this portion of the voyage is performed during the migration of quails immense numbers will fly on board, even in sufficient quantities to feed a ship's company. When on board the old government troop-ship, Urgent, close to Pantaleria, a sudden change of wind brought up a disagreeable ground-swell, and the old vessel pitched about in that lumbering manner peculiarly her own. Quail had been seen during the early part of the day, but they had passed onwards disregarding us; but the change of wind caused them now to act differently, for the new breeze was an adverse one, and the little travelling strangers were glad to rest their wearied wings upon our decks. Poor little creatures, so fatigued were they that without an effort they permitted themselves to be taken.

Although I consider Valetta the prettiest city with which I am acquainted and one of the very pleasantest

F

places to pass a month or two of winter in, it is without exception, as far as field sports go, the worst station it has been my lot to visit. True, at certain times a few migratory birds can be killed, but success is so uncertain that one can never be sure of obtaining sport.

For yachting and boating Malta is eminently suited. At the same time it must not be imagined that it never blows there—aye, it does blow; and the most veteran sailor must acknowledge that there are pleasanter positions than being caught in a *gregale:* however, they do not last, but are proportionably violent to the shortness of their existence. One January afternoon I left Malta on board a small vessel; the wind was fair, and with all the canvas we could set, merrily and swiftly we increased the distance between ourselves and land. When the sun set, the sky foretold no indication of change; still at midnight we were lying-to under a close-reefed mainsail, with a wild and broken sea every few minutes making a breach over us. In four hours the squall had subsided, and day broke clear and tranquil, while the coast of Sicily, smiling in its luxuriant vegetation and dotted with white cottages, lay close to windward. But during that squall we lost a hand overboard, a fair-haired boy, from fourteen to fifteen years old, the favourite of all. Poor lad! with others of his watch, he was sent to stow the jib, the craft pitched heavily into an unusually large sea, and he was hurried prematurely into a sailor's grave. Alas! such is life; while in the possession of the most robust health, how often are we close to the destroyer!

CHAPTER VII.

AN INDIAN HUNTING ENCAMPMENT.

LET others boast and proudly toast
    The light of ladies' eyes,
And swear the rose less perfume throws
    Than beauty's fragrant sighs;
The ripe, red lips in hue eclipse
    The ruby's radiant gem,
That woman's far the brightest star
    In Nature's diadem.
Yet since, for me, no charms I see
    In all the sex can show,
And smile and tear alike appear,
    And heedless flash or flow,
I'll change my theme, and fondly deem—
    True sportsmen pledge me here,
And fill my cup, and drain it up,
    To saddle, spur, and spear.

But while I sing, Time's rapid wing
    This lesson seems to teach—
The joy and bliss of sport like this
    Are still within our reach.
Then let's away at break of day,
    Ride vale and hill-top o'er,
Scale mountain's side, or stem the tide,
    To spear the flying boar.

> And Time may then bring love again,
>   When we at pleasure's shrine,
> To check his flight for one gay height
>   Will wet his wing with wine;
> And ere we part pledge hand and heart
>   Once more to rally there,
> To fill the cup, and drain it up,
>   To saddle, spur, and spear.
>
> *Indian Hunting Song.*

HAVING been knocked about in different portions of the globe principally on active service, during which my time was fully engaged with business which almost excluded me from field sports, quite three years must be jumped over between the events that I am about to tell of and those of a previous chapter.

With what pleasure, on obtaining leave of absence, did I look forward to the holidays, when again my gun would become my companion, more especially as India was to be the scene! The start at length was made; the sun shone bright and strong, but ere the journey to my intended shooting-ground had been accomplished, a break took place in the weather, which almost induced me to abandon the expedition.

With the mind vacillating between doubt and hope, I slowly made my way through the pitiless, pelting storm, hoping ere night to come across some native village, from whence I could obtain the information that would lead me to our encampment. The ardour of the chase had led me thoughtlessly forward, neglecting to take notice of the landmarks, and when at last I became thrown out by the boar taking shelter in a thick cover that edged an extensive ravine, I desired to return. North, south, east, and west, all appeared the same, and I had not the slightest idea in what direction to urge my horse. Worse than all, my situation was rendered doubly miserable by one of those pelting tropical showers coming on, that so frequently take place at the change of the monsoon, beating the poor verdure with such terrible force that it is only a wonder that each leaf and blade of grass can resist being forced into the bowels of the earth. My poor horse Hamet, who, in the morning, had been all life, fire, and courage, was now fatigued and crestfallen, and but that I occasionally touched his snow-white flanks with my sharp persuaders, and shook him up with the bit, he would doubtless have fallen. I managed, however, to keep moving, each flash of lightning causing him to start with fear, so vivid and near approached the electric fluid. At length the torrent of rain began to slacken, and I was looking forward to the far from enviable position, "a night's bivouac in a strange neighbourhood," abounding with beasts of prey, when my eyes were gladdened and my spirits restored by a sight of three white tents snugly nestling under the shade of a grove of banians, with several horses picketed at regular intervals. I was well aware that countrymen only could be their occupants, and without hesitation determined, according to the hospitable habits of the East, to demand both shelter and food for man and beast. No sooner thought than done; I directed my course to the largest tent, and, dismounting from my nag and slipping the snaffle-rein over my arm, I called for a horse-coolie, when, who should pop out his head through the fly-door but my jolly, good-tempered friend Steer. I had not seen him for more than two years, and on that occasion we parted in Paris, little expecting that the next time we met would be under an Indian sky. For some time neither spoke, so great was our mutual astonishment, but as soon as he had recovered his powers of utterance, he welcomed me, and would hear of nothing else than a promise to remain and join their party for the few remaining days of their hunt. After a due amount of hallooing, a syce* put in his appearance, to whose care my gallant steed was entrusted, with a caution that if a soil or mark of the day's travel should be found on him on the morrow, the groom's dusky hide would be tanned into leather and his life be considerably jeopardized. Inside I was introduced to Barker and McCarthy, both of whom I had frequently heard of as the hardest riding and most indefatigable sportsmen in the Presidency. Soon I effected a change of raiment; one supplying me with unmentionables, another a coat, and so on, each vieing with the other who could do the most for the unexpected visitor. "Where are you come from?" "Where are you going?" "How did you come here?" "Take a drink?" "Have a smoke?" "What shall it be, brandy or sherry?" &c., &c., &c., were showered upon me as quick as each could talk, giving me not a chance to slip in a word even edgeways. As a final chance, and running a risk of being deemed rude, I called them to order, and obtained an opportunity to explain myself. Steer, with his

* Native groom.

usual consideration, calling to the boy who had charge of the commissariat department to supply me with a stiff glass of brandy-pawnee and a cheroot, having a most astute knowledge of what would be beneficial and enjoyable after my ducking. Soon my yarn was spun, and a courier despatched to inform my comrades of my safety, and with a request that they would strike camp and hurry up and join us. The rain now had entirely ceased, and as we sat down to dinner *al fresco*, all nature being invigorated, the green of the foliage was doubly brilliant, and each tree appeared to contain a perfect choir of songsters. What a jovial meal we had; game in profusion, potted meats, pickled lobster, and as fine a mango-curry and mullagatawny soup as ever graced the board of a Governor-General! Then the fruits and wines—Madeira that had twice doubled the Cape, luxurious port and claret, almost as old as ourselves, and brandy not a whit younger, with an inexhaustible store of Schweppe's incomparable soda-water. If we indulged, who could be so hardhearted as to condemn? The conversation turned on the absorbing subjects, the horse, hound, spear, and rifle. My hosts had been out for some weeks, but their desire for sport had not yet flagged, although they had killed an immense quantity and variety of game. The following day had been set aside by them for the destruction of an enormous boar, who for months had roamed the neighbourhood, making sad havoc among the natives' sugarcane, a terror to all, and not unlike Alexander Selkirk, monarch of all he surveyed, but, with a great dislike to society, which he, without reluctance, showed to any unfortunate darkie whom chance threw in his way. Over and over again our glasses were filled, deeds of prowess were recounted, and as the generous wine began more freely to circulate, loose reins were given to both our tongues and imaginations, and I have little doubt, if an outsider could have heard our conversation, he would have put us all down for the veriest set of braggarts that ever stretched their limbs under mahogany. At length wine was discarded as too washy, and the more potent and ever popular brandy-and-soda circulated in place. The programme of to-morrow was not forgotten, and if we could have been taken at our word, no knight of old or gallant crusader could have performed greater or more perilous deeds than the happy quartet there assembled. To bed we no doubt got, but how? is the question; nevertheless we found ourselves with throbbing heads and feverish pulses awake at break of day, very desirous of a dash of brandy in our coffee, or, still better, a goodly draught of hock and seltzer-water. It has been frequently and well stated that there is no rest for the wicked, and doubtless we were classed in that category, for our attendants persisted in reminding us that our horses were saddled and the beaters and shikarees waiting. I had already exhausted my entire stock of ammunition in shape of bootjacks, boots, &c., that lay within reach, by throwing them at the intruders' heads, when I found that the incessant disturbance had driven the fickle Somnus from my embrace. To be up and doing was certainly better than restlessly kicking about under bedclothes; so I summoned my exhausted energy to the rescue and sprang from my couch. Little time was lost in donning my habiliments and gaining the open air.

Two of my friends I found on the ground; the third could not be drawn although several attempts were made, for he became pugnacious; so we determined to leave him behind, well knowing that an idle day in camp, with no associates and nothing to amuse him, would be a sufficient punishment.

On inspecting Hamet, I found that he had scarcely recovered from his previous day's fatigue, and as he was entered for several races at the cantonments and I had already backed him for a considerable amount I determined not to go. McCarthy, however, with the characteristic kindness of his countrymen, insisted that I should ride a horse of his, a young Australian thoroughbred, of great speed and beauty, that he had lately imported.

Without loss of time Goldfinder was led up, and all his owner said in his praise was but justice. The silky short coat, fine thin mane and tail, deep girth and broad chest, enormous hind-quarters, immensely muscular arms and small, flat legs, spoke doubtless of a pedigree without blot or stain. However, as I gloated over his fascinating shape, I could not help noticing a peculiar, devilish twinkle about his eyes, as the saddle was placed on his back, that practice and experience informed me denoted rather a queer temper. McCarthy observed my stare, and coolly remarked, with the utmost *sang froid*, " He's a trifle difficult to sit at first; but it's all over in a minute." Said McCarthy had hunted in his youth with the Blazers,* and considered anything rideable that

---

* A celebrated pack of foxhounds in Galway, whose supporters are noted for their hard riding.

could carry a saddle; consequently, he never had anything but vixens in his stable, for whenever he heard of a nag who had nearly or entirely killed his rider, or whom nobody could handle, and whom the happy possessor would sell for a song to be rid of, McCarthy came to the front and purchased him at his own price. The result was that he was better mounted, and that at a third of the money, than any other officer in the Presidency.

CHAPTER VIII.

FIRST BLOOD.

NOW as McCarthy's ideas on this subject were just mine, and as success had always gilded my efforts, I did not hesitate to try the issue. Without trouble I got up to the horse's withers, and with a vault put myself in the saddle. The groom, either out of ignorance or thinking I was seated, let go his head before I could get my feet in the irons, and a series of efforts was performed by the vicious animal that required all the nerve and pluck of which I was possessed to counteract. Of all the manœuvres that a wicked horse can practise, there are none so troublesome as buck-jumping. For the uninitiated, I will describe the operation. The horse hogs his back, springs rapidly, repeatedly, and perpendicularly into the air, lighting on all fours at the same moment, and, strange to say, the close tight seat, so much to be recommended generally, is here unavailing. For the very life of me I could not get my feet into the irons, and as I had been nearly unhorsed several times, I determined to become aggressor, and at least have the satisfaction of drawing blood, even if I did get a spill. My spurs were Latchford's best, and tolerably severe, and as my nag rose for a further essay, I sunk my toes and forced my heels well under and into his flanks. With a snort of pain and rage, he broke into a gallop, the very thing I desired, and without respite I kept him at top speed for at least a couple of miles. When I rejoined my *confrères* his glossy bay coat was lathered with sweat, his flanks heaved and nostrils stood expanded, but the viciousness had disappeared, and a very child might now have handled him. The effect of the excitement and the rapid passage through the air was most beneficial to myself, for the heated, feverish headache had disappeared, and I was rejuvenated. While my humbled steed underwent a scrape, I enjoyed an excellent cup of tea, which put me thoroughly to rights.

Our beaters and shikarees, from the lengthened delay, had become very impatient; so, to keep them in good humour, we started without further delay. Barker and McCarthy had the reputation of being second to none in this most exciting and often dangerous amusement, for both, on several occasions, had carried the spear of honour when with the Bengal Club—no small achievement among such noted sportsmen. For myself, this was nearly a maiden effort, and, from my late arrival, I was considered by both a "griffin," a favourite expression for a new arrival, or, more correctly, a green hand.

The morning, as is frequent after rain, was all that could be desired, cool, bracing, and invigorating, and merrily we chatted as we rode along, over open savannah covered with brush, or rolling hill-sides clothed with timber, every few steps flushing game, often brilliant in their resplendent plumage. Three or four miles brought us to the place where we intended commencing our beat. As far as I could judge the ground was most favourable ; a long valley, level at the bottom, densely planted with sugar-cane, with about a hundred yards of deep, thick jungle on either side, running along its entire length, which must have been quite a couple of miles. From the upper edge of the valley, on both sides, the plain stretched away for miles, and uninterrupted by anything large enough to deserve the denomination of a tree. In truth, after years of experience, I have never met a place so admirably adapted for our purpose as the Todah Valley. McCarthy soon gave the necessary instructions to the sable beaters, ordering them to go to the top of the ravine, and, extended at regular intervals like a company of skirmishers, beat it from end to end. While waiting to give them sufficient time to reach the place where they were to commence, a more picturesque sporting tableau could scarcely be conceived. Captain McCarthy —habited in a short fustian jacket, the colour of which nearly approached to the faded tints of withered herbage, his limbs encased in well-fitting, white buckskin breeches and boots, looked a perfect Apollo in form, though probably a little under medium height, his handsome sunburnt features radiant with expected excitement ; a fine specimen of a handsome, well-bred Irish gentleman—leant upon the neck of his noble horse, a perfect type of the high-class Arab ; while Barker was not one whit behind his friend in Nature's gifts, though of a totally different style. The Anglo-Saxon was strongly indicated in his laughing, fair countenance, lit up with the best-tempered pair of dark blue eyes, shaded with a profusion of fair, bright curly locks; his attire was of the same sporting cut and texture, only, if anything, a little more foppish; his steed was from the same desert regions, a perfect specimen of that justly-lauded breed. Two more daring or dashing soldiers or horsemen it would be difficult to find, and although years have passed since their life's blood was shed in their country's cause, their names still live in sporting circles as undoubted *noblesse* in the art of venerie. Poets and authors have lauded the Arab horse, and worthily does this most noble animal deserve all the praise that can be bestowed on him. For those who have not had opportunities of making his acquaintance, a few words of description may not be thrown away. Their general colour is white or gray, occasionally chesnut, and more rarely brown; height rarely exceeding fourteen hands and a half; broad, expanded forehead; remarkably large, bright, intelligent eyes; fine, tapering muzzle; immense nostrils and deep jowl; small pricked ears; thin withers; splendid shoulder; barrel-like carcase; very compact, muscular quarters; tail set very high and square, with legs beneath the knee flat as a board; though scarcely as fast as our best thoroughbreds, yet capable of occasionally doing their mile in 1·48, as the racing calendar of India will prove; but in addition to all these good qualities, they stand out paramount in docility, endurance, and courage, for they will face the fiercest beast of prey their rider can charge them at, relying entirely on the will and discretion of their jockey, a performance which I have seldom found an Australian horse equal to, and still less an English animal.

Half an hour must have elapsed when the distant sound of the beaters struck welcomely on the ear, and Captain McCarthy proposed an immediate taking to saddle and cessation of conversation. As we did not wish to separate, we determined all to remain on one side, as there was known to be quite a surplus of game on the beat, and if we failed to kill the veteran to-day, we should find sufficient to amuse us, and defer his fate to a future occasion. The Captain and Lieutenant—the latter was Barker's rank—were soon in the saddle; first having each carefully selected a spear from the half dozen carried by their favourite shikaree or constant hunting attendant, and calling on me to attend them, put their respective horses, Saltoun and Zampa, to a smart canter, striking for the edge of the ravine, where the brush looked thicker and more impenetrable. Louder and louder the discordant but still exhilarating cries of the beaters struck upon our impatient ears. Occasionally a more demonstrative shout would rise, indicating that the quarry was afoot and had been seen. With our nerves strung to the greatest possible tension, keeping the most profound silence, we awaited the result. An occasional rustling, or cracking of some withered limb, would place us upon the *qui vive;* but the sound would soon die away, telling that the intruder had preferred passing on, and retaining the shelter of the interwoven scrub to taking the open country. Step by step the beaters advanced, and the delay was becoming painful. The swarthy natives having nearly got abreast of our position, we were on the point of moving half a mile farther down, when, to our delight, a grizzled old veteran, his snow-white tusks and jaws bedaubed with saliva, rushed for the open, and with a speed perfectly astonishing for an animal of such ungainly and awkward proportions. Not one of us moved a muscle, well knowing if the boar became alarmed before he got some distance on the plain, he would probably return to the friendly shelter he had just left. On he went in a straight line, evidently determined to make for a belt of bush about three miles distant. As McCarthy detected growing indications of a desire for immediate pursuit, he begged that we would let the brute have a few minutes' more law, adding, *sotto voce*, " Perhaps when you get near him, the cultivation of his acquaintance may not be quite so desirable." At length, with one accord, pursuit was commenced, and settling myself down in the saddle, foot home in the stirrup, and nag well in hand, I settled into a slashing gallop. My mount was excessively restless, probably from his being frequently raced, and with all my exertion I could not get his head down. I was much lighter than my acquaintances, and that, in combination with the irregularity of the surface of the ground, gave me an immense advantage, so that, almost before I was aware of it, I was leading by several lengths. Even thus early my nag had made several stumbles from his stargazing propensity, but what to do ?—I would rather break my neck than pull up. I believe I would cheerfully have given a month's pay and allowances on a double batta station to have had on a martingale; however, I consoled myself that as some distance was yet to be travelled before I came alongside my antagonist, the fatigue would somewhat reduce the surplus fire in my now hateful mount. For the first half mile we did not appear to be overtaking our prey, but afterwards each stride visibly shortened the intermediate space, and, barring accident, I might expect soon to range alongside. Still my steed would keep his confounded snout in the air; every stratagem and effort I knew of was employed, yet I could not bring his head down to its proper place. Not more than seventy yards now intervened, and I had balanced my spear at the proper grip that I might the better be prepared for immediate action, when Goldfinder misplaced his foot and threw me forward on his withers. Would that I could have been striding my own tried and gallant little horse! If Richard offered his kingdom for a nag, I believe I would have given my commission, which, to me, was equally valuable. Although I had lost several lengths by the stumble, I was soon back in my saddle, and dashing along at the same break-neck pace. Whenever I could spare my eyes from my horse I fixed them on the boar. He was still running fresh and apparently unfagged, an occasional grunt of defiance from him striking upon my ear, sounding as if my foe was throwing back a challenge. Suddenly the quarry's stride became contracted, and, with his feet well under him, he made a splendid leap over something —what it was, I could not see.

G

CHAPTER IX.

A SHARP BURST.

AS it is a current saying that "whatever a hog can get over, a horse will have no difficulty in flying," any idea of shirking the leap never entered my head. Getting my mount in hand a little better, as a necessary caution, I ran Goldfinder at it, about the same spot that the boar had taken; my nag still had his head turned to the skies in search of stars, which he was destined to make both his rider and self see before many moments. To say that he jumped, or made any alteration in his gait, would be simply untrue; at the same pace he was going, and as if no such place existed, he dropped into the dry crack (for such it was, an obstacle of frequent occurrence throughout the arid plains of India), sending me head-foremost on the opposite side, and making me more suddenly and less ceremoniously acquainted with mother earth than I ever hope to be again; however, I received no more serious damage than the loss of some hide off the prominent portions of my physiognomy, and with as much rapidity as I could command picked myself up, that I might be certain of securing my detestable Bucephalus before he had gained his pins. I had not a moment to spare, for he was already half out, and but that the reins had got turned over his head when I got the somersault, I might not have succeeded. So rapidly had the whole scene passed that my friends had only obtained a slight lead, so a sudden turn or trifling mishap might yet give me a chance of first blood. Without waiting to see what injury the horse had suffered, I sprung upon his back, and, barring that he moved a little stiff for the first few strides, an outsider could not have remarked any difference. From leading the hunt, I now had the pleasure of whipping up the ruck—a place little to my satisfaction. Master piggy had, so far, not shown any signs of fatigue, and his steady gait and measured stride were indications of an indomitable spirit and formed determination of fighting the enemy whenever they encroached upon his route, or attempted to impede his progress. Barker led McCarthy by some lengths, but a few strides more would range the leading horseman alongside, and he had already poised his spear and taken his horse to the left, so as to deliver the honoured thrust with decision, when his bright spurs struck the flank of his gallant Arab, who, nobly answering the call, put on an additional burst, and the next moment the glittering keen weapon was passed through the hog's flank; but the thrust was only a flesh-wound. Some irregularity in the pace of the horse, or a sudden swerve in the boar, caused the weapon to slant, and instead of going in between the shoulder-blades and descending, it had glanced off the right shoulder-blade, and, penetrating through several inches of flesh and hide, had come out beneath. This wound, although a ghastly one, was not necessarily mortal, and as the successful sportsman parted with his weapon, the boar charged to the left, and, but for the agility of his horse and the promptness of his bridle-hand, would probably have succeeded in effecting damage. Barker was now disarmed, and therefore no longer able to give assistance. He had had the honour of first spear, but in taking that had become *hors de combat*. McCarthy and self therefore only remained to finish the drama, and the uncertain disposition of my horse rendered my service, in case of emergency, not much to be trusted. The hog's deviation enabled me to cut off an angle, and, if the Captain failed, an opportunity for redeeming myself would be at hand. The pace of our quarry had become considerably slackened; the wound and loss of blood were telling, and the inconvenience of ten feet of a male bamboo dangling from his brawny side was not calculated to improve at any time a doubtful temper. McCarthy raised himself in his stirrups, took a feeler on his horse's mouth, and being assured that all was right and that the gallant nag was ready for his share of the work, rushed him alongside and buried his blade deep in the infuriated victim's back; still, he did not fall, but after staggering a few paces, came to bay, steadying himself, to meet to the best advantage the first aggressor. "Neck or nothing!" I muttered between my compressed lips, and with an unexpressed but fervent desire that Goldfinder would go straight, I charged at my formidable adversary. The shock of the fall or the severity of the pace had been beneficial, for without a swerve my nag headed right at him, and as he rose to clear the hog with a jump, I struck well and home, but still too far in rear to have an immediate effect; however, I was pleased with the effort, for both McCarthy and Barker simultaneously exclaimed, " Well done !" The hog now squatted on his hams, turning his wicked small eyes, darting rays of hate, at his pursuers ; once he turned round, and, with an angry grunt, ground into shreds the tough spear handle which still adhered to him. McCarthy, however, was ready to go at him again ; a second time he reined his steed to the struggle, the boar staggered forward to meet him, but this last effort only hurried the execution of the death-warrant, for the skilfully-handled blade took the foe in front of the shoulder, and passing downwards pierced the heart. As our victim turned over on his flank, the death-halloo was sounded with all the energy that our united lungs could command, and numerous were the congratulations we exchanged on the successful termination of so hard-fought a battle.

Our horses had all suffered from the severity of the pace, and with one accord we dismounted to slacken girths and turn their heads to the wind, the better to enable them to enjoy any passing draught of air. On examining Goldfinder I found that his escapade in the ravine had not otherwise injured him than depriving him of some hair. The entire run from start to finish was now descanted on, and Barker received due praise for the honour he had earned in drawing first blood, or otherwise taking first spear. I could not forbear during this interval of relaxation from having a cut at McCarthy for the confounded brute he had lent me, adding that it was a mercy he hadn't broken my neck; in fact, I felt a little sore at his treatment, for assuredly I had never straddled such a dangerous, headstrong devil; but the gallant Captain soon explained all, and that to my satisfaction. He had had the horse in his stable for some months, and when he first procured him his conduct was similar to his performance of this day, but finding he had a bold and determined rider on his back, had gradually succumbed, and had performed on many late occasions most satisfactorily. The groom had, moreover, forgotten to put a ring on one of the reins; and although Goldfinder's owner had noticed this, he had preferred not acquainting me with this apparently trifling piece of carelessness, fearing it would worry and annoy me, thereby taking much of my interest from the sport.

The motley crew of beaters at length came up, and numerous and various were their comments upon our success. One of the shikarees assured us that a larger and older boar had broken cover; but that after going a short way into the open, he became alarmed and returned, charging through their scattered ranks, to the dismay and trepidation of the sable crowd. As soon as our horses were refreshed, and the necessary instructions given for the transportation of our game to camp, we started on our return, deeming that our faithful steeds had worked enough for one day, and, as we had no remounts out, we would defer further execution till the morrow.

Indian scenery, with its too-frequently scorched

appearance, still has a fascination. The grass-covered plains, the broken ground, the magnificent giant trees, the solitary watercourses, always embanked with numerous flowering shrubs, together form a pleasant landscape; and although the sun may be oppressive and overpowering in its rays, its brightness still adds an essential without which the view of the most favoured portions of the globe would look sombre, gloomy, and depressing.

CHAPTER X.

THE STORM.

THE day was not far advanced when we reached our temporary forest home, lighthearted, joyous and thankful for the excellence of our run and the success of its termination. The fresh air had dissipated the fumes of our last evening's potations much more effectually and rapidly than any specific in the shape of draughts or correctives. Steer was still *en déshabillé*, and in far from an amiable frame of mind at not having witnessed what my friends concurred in calling the fastest and best run of the season. While we were fresh and hungry, anxious for some tiffin, he was fretful and peevish at having been left behind, to toss restlessly on his couch, without the benefit of the fresh air of morning and an opportunity of working off the effects of his nocturnal excesses. Tiffin was rapidly served and disposed of, and each betook himself to his favourite book and cigar to while away the remainder of the day. I have previously stated that we were under canvas in a beautiful grove, but the nature and lay of the ground requires fuller description, that after-events may be more easily understood. The ground on which we were encamped was level and smooth, covered with a close bottom of short grass, the result of the beneficial shade of the mammoth trees; fifty yards on the left there began a gradual ascent, covered with brush and interspersed with broken rock, gradually becoming more rough as the hill ascended, and ultimately terminating in a rocky bluff, fantastic and irregular in shape, the undoubted retreat of many a skulking jackal and hyena as well as of innumerable reptiles. McCarthy, as I heard afterwards, had objected to taking up his residence so near to a probable ambush, but the vicinity of water and the wishes of the attendants had combined to gain his consent. The afternoon turned out hot and sultry, the morning breeze subsiding into a calm; within doors, even with an attendant fanning you, but a limited amount of comfort could be enjoyed. We had expected that my companions would have arrived ere this, and, but that we wished to be on hand to welcome them, our pajamas * would have been donned, and a *siesta* attempted. However, at two o'clock, a chattering among the attendants proclaimed the advent of strangers; and Beamish, Peel, and Strangeways hove in sight. We were now a jolly party, seven in all, and while the servants were pitching new habitations their masters were pitching into the viands. A meeting such as this, in the greenwood glade or on the swelling prairie, has always its fascination;

---

* A light suit of flannel, generally slept in.

the farther from the haunts of countrymen the more warm you feel towards them if chance should bring you in contact. You pass a mere acquaintance with a nod of recognition in Regent Street, but if you should encounter him on the slopes of the Rocky Mountains or in the silent forests of the North West, you would hail his appearance with open arms.

There is nothing more lively and gay than the camp of the soldier or sportsman in tropical India; the hordes of attendants, of all classes, castes, sexes, and ages, all engaged in some occupation or another, for the Hindoo, unlike his European brother, strictly confines himself to one line of work, out of which he will not step unless absolute compulsion is used. Hence, while in other countries one or two attendants are all that is required, here it takes a dozen, more or less. Your groom would feel himself insulted if asked to look after your dogs, and your body-servant would never survive being sent to carry water. If you smoke a hookah, a boy is necessary to look after it and keep it in order. That which is no person's special business is soon neglected, while if you have a particular task allotted to each, they will generally faithfully attend to it. Again, around an European's encampment are numerous animals, such as horses, dogs, cattle, goats and sheep, besides pets in variety sufficient to stock a menagerie. However, the whole makes an effective picture, relieved and improved by the snow-white graceful garments of the natives. Moreover, they are a handsome race — perhaps a little effeminate in features, but their figures are invariably upright and well-proportioned, with a truly stately carriage. Dinner had

OUR CAMP.

been disposed of with the setting sun, and we all, with one accord, had seated ourselves outside our dining-tent. Days gone by and distant friends formed the principal topic of conversation, for we were unusually quiet, the heat having become oppressive in the extreme, and electricity surcharged the atmosphere. An unnatural and portentous stillness pervaded the scene, only occasionally broken by the shrill, strange cry of a description of lizard, the certain foreboder of rain. McCarthy had left us but a few moments when he returned, with the information that the barometer had fallen, and if not much mistaken we were destined to see an uncomfortable night; a hint like this from an old stager, was not to be despised, and soon a crowd of half-asleep and wholly unwilling natives were summoned to dig gutters, put up storm-ropes and ease the tent-poles, the further to guarantee the safety of our fragile dwellings in case we should be visited by a tornado. In the course of my experience I have never found anything more abominable, and many of our gallant soldiers doubtlessly think likewise, than being ruthlessly awakened from your peaceful slumbers by a wet tent flapping about your ears, having to grope your way from underneath the ruins, and, perhaps, standing in a state of semi-nudity, exposed to the sweeping blast and penetrating rain. Well was it that McCarthy had given us the hint, for within an hour the storm was upon us, giving no further warning than a deep muttering sound caused by its rapid approach.

Dry leaves, straw and all light substances, were caught up and wheeled into the air, with a quick spiral motion, as if by the action of innumerable little whirlwinds, although as yet not a breath of air is stirring around us; dark, black, impenetrable clouds rise over the tree-tops with a rapidity that shows the power of the propelling wind, and the faint light emitted by the stars is suddenly shrouded in total darkness: a sudden flash of livid lightning illuminates the heavens with a ghastly glare, its dazzling brilliancy causing all to close their eyes; a noise as of a thousand siege-guns rapidly follows, making the earth tremble with fear at the superlative voice of the angry thunder. No signal from peak of man-of-war could have been more rapidly answered, for ere the echoes had died away, the rain descended, with a violence and body little less than that of a cataract, while the wind tore round, indicative of a force irresistible. The trees groaned and lashed the air, rubbing their gigantic limbs together, and evincing a strong inclination to prostrate themselves before the power of the Omnipotent. The din, the noise and tumult, caused by the breaking branches and falling trees, combined with the appalling thunder and falling torrent, made a most impressive, grand, and awful scene. What man who is a witness to such terrific grandeur, can fail to be impressed, and more firmly believe in the omnipotence and overpowering strength of the Creator? How much better would it be for all of us if we would think, and cease less soon to forget the beneficial impressions produced on such occasions! Again and again the gale, with increased power, surges over the surface of the earth, and in each repeated effort increases in its violence till it appears impossible that aught can resist its influence. Still our tents remain standing, but wondrously changed in shape—now bellying out on one side as if they would burst, at the next moment contracting, causing the occupants to be in constant dread of a collapse. Nevertheless, the scene is not without a certain amount of satisfaction, and imparts the same feelings that the rage of the ocean arouses in a brave heart—an appreciation and admiration of its sublimity. But, fortunately, these tornadoes do not last long, and in a couple of hours from its advent it had passed away to leeward, leaving naught but the *débris* and our own memory to recall the episode. Although at the outset they cause discomfort and inconvenience, the after-results fully compensate; vegetation and animal life receive new vigour, the heated air becomes cool, and the breezes are loaded with fragrance emitted from the formerly parched flora; the whole woods are animated, insects, lizards, and tree-frogs emit their joyous, harmonious notes, the horses neigh, and the goats bleat, in probable anticipation of fresh and succulent herbage for their morning repast.

The effect was much the same on us frail mortals. Soon we were all congregated; our former depression of spirits had fled with the storm, our plans were laid for the morrow, and all, with the exception of Peel, determined to visit the Todah valley; he, however, had different views, and being the happy possessor of a newly-imported brace of pointers, resolved to devote himself to the pursuit of the feathered beauties. This gentleman, unfortunately for himself, was never a proficient in the saddle, and invariably preferred walking to straddling a horse. Hog-sticking he had attempted several times, but from his deficiency in equitation had received so many and such severe falls, that he was always glad to seize an excuse that would justify his backing out.

CHAPTER XI.

A VETERAN BOAR.

ALTHOUGH we all retired late, it did not prevent our putting in an early appearance next morning. The beaters who had to travel to the hunting-ground on foot were dispatched before daylight, and we followed them an hour afterwards. Our horses were all in excellent spirits, the freshness of the air and the previous day's rest having most advantageously told upon them, and not one iota less did their riders enjoy the atmospheric change. Our journey was pleasant and merry, each vieing with the other in loquacity and good-humour. Never can I look back on those pleasant times without regret, for they are probably passed never to be repeated. Who is there whose existence, however sad, has not some bright spot worthy of remembrance, that, when recalled, appears as an oasis placed in the middle of a desert! Near the scene of our previous day's exploits, we overtook our sable attendants, who mustered strong, thus increasing the prospect of good sport. Everything was suitable as far as weather was concerned—bright, cool and fresh, and the evening's shower had made the ground in much better order for galloping. As the number of horsemen was also increased, McCarthy, who was universally elected leader, decided that we should separate, and three take each side, while if we spread ourselves along the valley, we could still be within range of each other's vision, and at the same time afford less chance for any game that should be forced afoot getting an opportunity to escape without being seen. Peel had accompanied us thus far, but as we were detailed off for our different posts by our chief *pro tem.*, he started in an opposite direction, where, from the number of cultivated fields and the frequent occurrence of habitations, the best promise of feathered game was made.

Our disposition was as follows: McCarthy, Barker and self took the right side, while Strangeways, Beamish and Steer took the other. As I placed myself at my stand, nearly three-quarters of a mile below where the beaters first broke in, with the captain below me and the lieutenant above, I could not help thinking that the unfortunate piggy who attempted to cross the open to-day would stand an uncommonly good chance of becoming pork. Some time of utter silence slipped by, while I with sharp eye and quick ear tried to detect the slightest sound and note the most trifling movement; so far nothing had broke, unless it was some skulking jackal, or equally ignominious prowler. Again and again some imaginary noise had for the moment made me more alert, but as rapidly the false alarm subsided. The turmoil, proclaiming the distant advance of the beaters, was now borne upon the breeze; first, only an occasional shout of some more powerful and energetic member of the dusky crew, but at length the noise of all was distinctly heard, like the babbling of a distant pack. As I have the heart to love all kinds of field sports, such a scene as the present was most enjoyable; for although none of the larger game were in sight, but few moments elapsed without crowds of the feathered denizens of the forest being disturbed and compelled to take wing from their shady retreats. The peacock, grand in size and gorgeous in plumage; the jungle fowl, doubtless the original of our domestic poultry, yet the wildest and most difficult of approach of all small game; the crow pheasant (a member of the cuckoo family), and numerous others, whiz past, all offering tempting shots, but with nothing but a hog spear they might almost roost upon my horse's mane with impunity. The second cheroot had been consumed, and impatience began to manifest itself, when a shout from Barker roused me from my lethargy. "Look out! look below there!" And look out I did. My position was well selected, for I could command a good view without being much exposed; I turned my gaze upwards towards the direction from whence the beaters were advancing, still nothing showed. I was just about to mutter, "What abominable luck! just as usual," and so on, when the sudden pricking of my horse's ears, and a certain nervousness of his manner, caused me to look to the right, and there, stealing away like a fox from cover, was the largest and most formidable boar I had ever yet seen. I was on the point of shouting the view hallo, but for fear that he had not got far enough, and might be prompted, if then disturbed, to make a retrograde movement, I kept silent. As soon as I dared, without fear of alarming my antagonist, I jumped to the ground, and, with the rapidity of a groom, took up a couple of holes in my girths, for well I knew they must be slack from the length of time that had elapsed since the saddling had taken place, and more than extra care was wanted to cope successfully with a grizzly savage of such formidable dimensions. With nervous hold I closed my knees as I re-seated myself, and with comparatively slack rein gave head to my clever little horse, who soon settled down to a steady three-quarter gallop. "Now, boys," I said to myself, "it will take a good man to deprive me of first blood." There was no fear now of the quarry returning, so I gave vent to my overstrung feelings with a joyous "tally ho." O, McCarthy! thou prince of sportsmen! few have ever been seen like thee before or since. Thy eye was sharp as the hawk's, thy ear quick as the kangaroo's! That one shout was sufficient to give him warning, and before I had got two hundred yards from my destined prey, I was aware that he was thundering after me. I had no longer the whole performance to myself—a false step, a heavy stumble, or perchance a fall, would give the gallant Captain a fair show for first blood, but still he should not have it if bold riding and willingness to dare aught would bestow it upon me. The ground was admirable, smooth and elastic; a few strides more would bring me alongside. Hold up, my gallant little horse, serve me well this time, and you shall have the first place in my affections ever after. Closer and closer I approach, with the reins well and firm in my bridle-hand; when I lift my steed as to a jump, drawing the claret at the same moment with my persuaders, and as I do so, with a well-directed thrust I bury the laurel-leaf-shaped spear-head deep in the brawny shoulder of the patriot boar, and ere he could revenge the insult, I was out of reach of his formidable tusks. I could have shouted—I believe I did. I had taken the spear of honour in the face of the acknowledged best hog-sticker in the Presidency. I've had various streaks of good luck in my life, with various joyous sensations, among which I may reckon the feelings of satisfaction each time that I saw my promotion in the "Gazette;" the feelings of internal pride when I first donned my uniform; my first successful essay on the racecourse; but all fell far short of my satisfaction at this moment: and as I wheeled round with the intention of administering the *coup de grâce*, I felt little ambition to dispute with McCarthy the honour of terminating the drama. The boar, as I struck him, charged to the left, but the agility of my horse had prevented this manœuvre from being effective. Being thus foiled in his intent, Master Piggy continued his course almost at right angles to that which he had previously pursued, and thus afforded my friend a better opportunity of coming in early to join in the *mêlée*. In hog-hunting I have invariably found that if the quarry change the direction of his flight from compulsion or an acquaintance with steel, he afterwards continues for some distance his new course. The Captain was now many strides nearer than myself, but the excitement of the run had put my nag upon his mettle, and as I directed him again to his work, his ardour and spirits knew no bounds, for with each stride he bore so upon his bit as almost to pull me out of the saddle; however, there was little need for any further assistance, for McCarthy, ranging alongside, struck strong and true, and though the hog continued about fifty paces farther, the blood streaming from his mouth, he gradually relaxed his pace, and, stumbling over an irregularity in the ground, fell to rise no more. On returning to the cover, we found that Barker was busily employed about half a mile off, and, before we could join him, had numbered another of the tusked gentry with the "have beens." Our horses were still fresh, and we were anxious for more work; nor were we long disappointed, for a few minutes after a "sounder" broke cover, under the leadership of a gaunt flat-sided old lady. The young ones were scarcely half-grown, so that their worthy mamma became the only object of attention, and a spirited race took place. The difference of weight was in my favour, if not the speed of our nags, for by the time I had drawn first blood, after a sharp burst of three quarters of a mile, I led the gallant Captain by ten lengths. Barker also had cut in and brought up the rear a good third, and to him fell the honour of dealing the death-blow. This second essay had blown both horses and riders, and as we dismounted and slackened girths, we agreed over our cigars that enough is as good as a feast; so that when the beaters joined us, and had received the necessary instructions for the finding of the different victims, we started for home in the best possible spirits at the result of our forenoon's performances.

We reached our jungle encampment glittering in the sun, for the luminary was now high in the heavens, and the reflected heat from the warmed earth was already becoming oppressive; our adventures of the morning had whetted our appetites, and a substantial tiffin, washed down with an abundance of Allsop's pale ale, soon satisfied the inward man; the cool spring near which we were situated having previously afforded each a luxurious bath. The desire to know the success of the rest of the party prevented us doubtlessly from taking a siesta; they did not come, and one by one we dropped off to our respective dormitories to enjoy our *otium;* probably *sine dignitate.* Well it was we did so, for neither Peel nor the others turned up till the long shadows of the evening proclaimed a termination of day. In his hurry to get divested of his equipments, Peel fastened his pointers, coupled together, to an unused tent-peg some fifty paces off, till his dog-coolie returned (who was temporarily absent), that he might the better join in discussing the day's work. The other trio had numerically been more successful than ourselves, but all that they had killed were small, while a large boar, which from their description must have been as big as a jackass, made good his escape. Our gunner had also a heavy bag, and visions of *fricassée* and "spatchcock" floated before our imaginations for the morrow's breakfast. Scarcely time for a change of raiment had elapsed when dinner was announced, and what our service and table lacked in equipments, was amply made up in the abundance and variety of dishes. Again and again the social bottle passed round the table, and as we were to separate on the morrow for different sections of the country, healths, good wishes, and future meetings were drunk; but hark! what is that unearthly shout? What on earth is that row? Our native attendants come tumbling into our tent as unceremoniously as if an evil spirit were after them. Not a word of satisfaction can we obtain; the entire crowd are terror-stricken and dumb, and the only sound that now strikes the ear is a most unearthly, discordant howling of a dog. At length, one more courageous than his fellows utters the dreaded word "bagh!" and the dusky crew seem to cower still more at the temerity of the speaker. None of us required further information; no "griffin" is up country a week but knows that this is native language for tiger. With a simultaneous impulse each seizes whatever weapon he can lay his hand on; fortunately, several double rifles, already loaded, hang against the tent-pole, and arming ourselves with them, we rush to the scene of action. The moon had now risen bright and clear, still nought could be seen; only the painful howling of a dog is heard on the hill-side not over two hundred yards from the camp. What can it mean? Where are the pointers? The whole scene flashed upon us like a dream. The unlucky dogs had been left out, and a hungry tiger had pounced upon them, carrying off one bodily, and dragging the other unfortunate by the coupling strap attached to his now, doubtlessly, dead companion. All were in a state of excitement; Peel stamped and swore, and acted like a maniac; the younger portion proposed an immediate pursuit, while McCarthy, long accustomed to all the mishaps of the hunting-field, in a cool but stern voice requested those who had not yet procured guns to do so without delay. Still we could hear the painful howling of the unfortunate canine, decreasing in volume and frequency as it was dragged farther and farther up the rugged hill-side. The suspense was awful, but, fortunately short, for soon all were on the spot, armed with either rifle or shot-gun loaded with ball. The fate of the unfortunate dog was truly tragical. His comrade no doubt had been killed in a moment, but for the survivor to be thus dragged, without the power of resistance, to certain death, from the midst of his friends and protectors, without a chance of escape, was truly horrible. With strict injunctions to keep together and act in unison, with a number of the most trustworthy natives, each carrying a lighted brand snatched from the camp fire, we all start, the plaintive moaning of the unfortunate pointer being our guide; luckily the cover was sparse, still the bloodthirsty brute could travel even with such a clog attached to him faster than we could advance, but McCarthy had little doubt, if we pressed on, that the destroyer would be kept too much occupied to mutilate his living victim. It was with difficulty that Peel could be kept back, each howl seemed to imbue him with fresh frenzy to wreak vengeance on the despoiler, and as argument became useless we had to resort to force. At length we gained the crest of the ridge, and from the distinctness of the less-frequently repeated howls, were evidently nearer the marauder. "On, on, boys!" was the word; "we're gaining on him; give him no rest. See! what is that? don't you perceive?" Something white is rushing towards us, and, wonderful to say, the lost dog bounded into our midst; never was a friend received with greater pleasure and ecstasy, all crowded around him anxious to pat or caress one who had almost risen from the dead ; nor was the poor brute's glee a bit less demonstrative, and scarcely could he stand still a moment to be looked at ; however, his collar was off, and doubtlessly in the rough handling he received it had slipped over his head.

CHAPTER XII.

THE SEARCH FOR THE MURDERER.

MANY hours elapsed, after reaching the tents, before our excitement subsided. Peel still continued half crazed at the loss of his dog, and vowed vengeance on the morrow upon the whole cat tribe for having deprived him of the services of so valuable a servant, and we all with one accord determined to brave the displeasure of our respective commanding officers rather than permit our friend to attempt alone so dangerous an undertaking as hunting out the midnight marauder. Long were the hours we sat discussing the matter and our intended method of proceeding, and when we separated to retire to our respective couches the wee small hours of the morning had arrived, guns had been cleaned, fresh ammunition sought out, and everything attended to which could ensure success. McCarthy attempted to induce some of our attendant peons to go and warn the neighbouring villagers that their services would be required to assist in destroying the prowling savage, but neither threats nor promises availed—all had been too much alarmed to venture forth from the safety of the encampment into the darkness; we had therefore to rest satisfied with the promise of two of the shikarees to start as soon as the first haze of dawn indicated the approach of day. The break of morning is generally the safest hour for travelling in such localities as are inhabited by beasts of prey, for generally long ere then they have satisfied their appetites, and are skulking home to hide themselves in the solitude of their dens, as if ashamed of their bloodthirsty avocation. On the morrow, when we marshalled, all armed to the teeth, and prepared for any emergency, quite a host of darkies were on the ground, no less anxious for success than ourselves, for many a straggler from their flocks had lately disappeared, and the fragments found afterwards removed all doubt of their fate. The destruction of cattle in some parts of India, through the attacks of wild animals, is so enormous as to be incredible; even the number of human beings carried off is far from small.* In the colony of Singapore and vicinity, where spices and other shrubby plants are cultivated, it is estimated that not less than one human being per diem meets with an untimely end from tigers; in fact, the natives are so much in dread of their visits and audacity that they build their dwellings upon poles, which elevate their houses from twelve to fifteen feet above the level of the ground. However, it is seldom in India that a tiger takes to homicide until he becomes old and effete, in fact

* In one district, from official returns in three years, over three hundred natives and five thousand cattle were killed by tigers.

unable to capture more active prey; but when once he has tasted human flesh, he prefers this description of food to all others. He haunts fords, neighbourhoods of public thoroughfares, or wells, and pounces upon the unsuspecting traveller or letter-carrier, in almost every instance with success. Many are the villages that have become partially depopulated and ultimately deserted because a man-eater has taken up his residence in their vicinity. A curious result is said to follow from this dietary. The criminal, after living for some months in this manner, becomes subject to hide-disease or mange, which, from the loss of hair and skin eruptions, makes his pelt almost useless.

Seven well-armed Europeans, each provided with a couple of double-barrels, and, from constant practice, nearly all good shots, were a formidable array, and the probability was if the foe showed himself that this day would terminate his career; however, nothing must be done rashly, for numerous are the fatal accidents that have resulted in following this sport. A tiger, however severely wounded, and on the verge of death, from his enormous strength and activity can, with one blow, finish any man's earthly career. A few years ago a work was published, written by Lieutenant Rice, of the Indian Army, who for a long period was the most successful tiger-slayer in that distant land; and he, nearly in every instance, followed the sport alone, as far as his own countrymen were concerned, only using a few of the natives as beaters, and success always attended him. Those desirous of information upon this dangerous description of shooting would do well to read his work, and learn how one cool and determined person obtains success. Another peculiarity which is worthy of noting in reference to this subject is that smooth-bore guns loaded with ball are frequently used. This, probably, can best be accounted for from the denseness of the cover in which the haunts of the prey are found, and the necessary short range at which your shots are fired.

After a lengthened consultation with the principals of the assembled natives, it was decided that a neighbouring nullah was the probable lair, and, as the distance to this retreat was little over half a mile, the services of our horses were dispensed with. Arriving at the ground, the situation, as far as human judgment could form an opinion, appeared just suited to form a welcome shelter; precipitous banks, overgrown with dense, tangled brush, and covered with innumerable giant boulders, formed many a sheltered nook and cranny, well screened from the oppressive rays of the vertical sun. This nullah, a couple of years before, had been the selected retreat of one of these tyrants. He had paid the penalty of his crimes, and up to the present time the ravine had been free from these scourges, but it was not unlikely that his successor, who had adopted the same nefarious line of business, had taken possession of the defunct tiger's premises. Our beaters did their work manfully, and, in spite of briars and other obstacles, scoured thoroughly the whole *locale*, but not a symptom of the presence of our foe could be found, so that after an hour's fruitless labour, disappointed in the results, we had to desist. Again a council of war was held, and a second similar retreat in the vicinity was pronounced as the most probable holding-place; but the result was a blank. The oppressive heat, the exertion of walking, and possibly the desire for breakfast, induced a unanimous decision for a temporary cessation of hostilities, on the express stipulation that all should join in making a further essay in the afternoon. In the meantime natives were despatched a few miles round the neighbourhood to glean what information could be obtained. Breakfast had been disposed of, and scarcely had we smoked our first cheroot sufficiently low to deserve the appellation of stump, when a courier arrived with the news that he had discovered in the sand surrounding a spring, three or four miles off, undoubted footprints. Boot and saddle were now proclaimed, and immediately afterwards, all mounted, were again *en route* to the expected rencontre. With what anxiety we all dismounted and inspected the tell-tale tracks! The signs were unmistakable and fresh, while the shikarees, who are skilled in such indications, pronounced that they had been made the previous night; doubtlessly the animal had washed down his feast of dog-meat at this pool before laying up for the day. On more closely examining the ground, old signs were also found so numerous that little doubt remained in our minds that this was a chosen resort after midnight excursions, and further convinced us that the brute was not far distant, for generally carnivora select a retreat within a short distance of water, and invariably slake their thirst at the same place.

Several pieces of dense thicket were in the vicinity, all of which were carefully searched, but still without results;

and despair had almost again taken possession of us when a native was seen swinging his puggree (the cloth which they tie round their heads) in the air, and violently gesticulating from a neighbouring height. This exhibition acted like a talisman, for all well knew that it indicated good news, and those who had commenced to lag and predict failure now sharpened up their pace, and vied with their comrades in obtaining the news. If we had been unsuccessful in viewing the game, we found that we had unkennelled it, for the tiger, alarmed by the approach of so many, and the noise made by the beaters, had thought proper to steal off, but, fortunately, had been viewed by this field-telegrapher, who had marked him down into a ravine not over half a mile from our present position. With strong hopes of at last gratifying our revenge, we hurried forward, and ere we arrived at the designated place, a second native confirmed the statement of the first, for he had not only seen the tiger into the nullah, but even pointed out his track on a bare piece of sandy soil. The locality was found to be admirably suited for our purpose, so that, if the foe had not passed on, we felt convinced that he could not a second time escape our vigilance. McCarthy disposed each with the discretion of an old hand, and, as the thicket did not cover more than an acre, all were within hailing distance in case of a view hallo or accident. The preconcerted signal having been given, the beaters, with heart and soul, went to their work, and amid shouts and threats of vengeance, steadily advanced towards the position of the guns. On, on they came, and the excitement of all was intense. Every muscle and nerve was strung to the utmost tension. A few moments more would proclaim the result; each man stood with his double-barrel, full cock, ready to send a leaden messenger at the hateful canicide. But half of the cover now remained, still nought had been seen, when a shot announced that something was afoot. The oft-repeated echoes had scarcely ceased reverberating when a second fire, from a different quarter, proclaimed that more than one eye had seen the quarry; and that the villain was a skulking coward—by far the most dangerous description—who knew too much to leave the friendly shelter. Again and again the shouts and derisive jeerings of the sable attendants rose as they forced their way forward; yet, still no further chance of a shot was afforded. So far only those that had fired knew what it was at, and the less fortunate were blaming their want of luck. However, a change soon came over the scene, and lively work followed the prolonged inaction. At a point covered by three guns, forth rushed a full-grown panther. Four shots turned him over ere he had gone ten paces, but soon he was up, and, nothing daunted, continued his forward course; ten strides farther would bring him upon Steer, who only now had one loaded barrel. His gun was pitched forward, and as his tube vomited forth its contents, a cross shot from Barker struck the foe in the loins, and he rolled over to rise no more. This fusilade had brought the whole of our party together, when, to the surprise of all, Strangeways announced that he had fired at a tiger, and not at the defunct. This put a new phase upon the play, and the temporarily deserted posts were again manned, the beaters ordered to recommence from the farther end, and afresh scour the thicket with renewed energy and racket. But all was no avail; the striped beauty had taken advantage of the opportunity and escaped, possibly to fall at some future date before another's rifle.

CHAPTER XIII.

THE TIGER'S DEATH.

THERE are no people on the face of the earth so capable of bearing fatigue as the lower caste natives of India; no day appears too long, no journey too far for their agile frames, and the velocity with which they advance is truly surprising; frequently have I ridden nine or ten miles within the hour, yet, when I halted, my faithful syce was not far distant. Now, what do you think they live on, to render them capable of enduring, without fatigue, such great exertions? Beef, you might imagine, or some other equally strong food; no! nothing but vegetable diet, except in rare cases.

As the beaters entered the cover, one would have thought that they were fresh men, instead of being lately so constantly worked, so great was their energy and desire to see the marauder slain, and no doubt the possibility of having a chance of singeing their inveterate enemy's whiskers,* acted as no mean stimulant.

* Immediately on the death of a tiger the natives singe his whiskers, believing it to be the greatest insult they can offer their bloodthirsty foe.

I

I particularly observed from the first one dusky, handsome peon, who acted as an accepted chief among his sable associates, and from appearance and bearing was well qualified to fill so important a post. I had noticed him always the first to enter cover, and if a symptom of reluctance or fear showed itself among the others, he, in few words, ridiculed and laughed them out of their timidity. All the natives carried some weapon, many matchlocks,* but in his powerful hand he held a keen-bladed tulwar,† which, doubtless, he could handle with effect.

The crew of beaters, as they pushed on, continued to shout incessantly. Their previous exertions, even under a vertical sun, had not impaired their *vim*. Forward, forward they advance, while my sporting companions remain mute as death—nervously each clasps his trusty weapon; twice a breaking branch or unexpected sound caused a looked-for advent of game. Not fifty yards now separate the representatives of the two nationalities, and the quarry has not shown itself; even the rustling of the beaters' steps can be distinctly heard, when, stealthily, slowly, crouching, with belly almost to the ground, and step as silent as that of a flitting phantom, advances from the brush the disturber of our previous evening's peace, his eyes livid with hate and fury; but in a moment he appears to comprehend the dangers of his situation, for, halting momentarily, he turned to regain

* Matchlocks are long-barrelled awkward guns, fired by means of a lighted fuse, which is pushed into a pan containing priming, after the manner of flint guns.

† Tulwar, a very keen-edged scimitar-shaped blade, in the use of which some of the natives are great proficients.

the friendly cover; but the pause had been sufficient to afford time for aim—three guns speak almost together, and with deep-muttered growl as he retires, two rugged bullets pierce his brilliantly-coloured coat; mischief now is in the wind, for, after blood has been drawn, the most adventurous and hazardous had better look well to their future proceedings.* Experience informed us that our swarthy attendants were now in imminent danger; though he would not face the sahibs'† bullets, the dark-skinned natives would stand less ceremonious treatment. Above the ordinary sounds made by the advancing peons rises a shout of extraordinary shrillness, and from my position numerous white-turbaned, white-clothed figures are seen to ascend the scattered saplings, while a wail of anguish issues from their vicinity. This indication is plain, and difference of language fails to prevent a full comprehension that some tragedy is being enacted. Each sportsman rushes from his post to the scene of discord, determined to do all, to brave aught, and bring assistance to whoever has been seized by the savage brute; but all were too late, for the marauder, who had seized the intrepid fellow whom I had previously mentioned, had been satisfied to give him but one blow with his powerful paw, and a sample of his teeth on the shoulder, afterwards dropping his victim and continuing his retreat.‡ We found poor Nana

* The majority of tigers, when hunted, will, if possible, steal off, but once they are wounded, they will attack indiscriminately man or beast that has the misfortune to come in their way.

† The correct meaning of this word is master, but the natives make general use of it in speaking of Europeans.

‡ Such an occurrence as this is extremely common, and the number of maimed hunters to be met who have received their wounds in similar ren-

Aboul dreadfully shaken and badly lacerated, but his heart and presence of mind had not left him; and as we bent over his prostrate figure examining and directing so as to afford assistance to the noble fellow, with glistening eyes and smiling countenance he rejoicingly articulated that he had not succumbed without testing the keenness of his tulwar across the muscular forearm of his assailant. His weapon, which he still retained in his nervous grasp, proved his assertion, for a crimson stain was on its bright blade. Having given orders to have Nana conveyed out of further danger, we re-established our cordon of beaters, and having been assured by our horse-coolies who remained between this cover and retreat that he had not left, with no lack of former *élan* and determination we resumed our work.

Our men had not proceeded over thirty paces, after turning to the right-about, when an angry growl sent them to tree, and many an excited voice proclaimed that the game was in sight, and determined to retreat no farther. Knowing our people to be safe, we now collected and advanced in mass, McCarthy and Barker forming the centre and front. Still we could see nothing; only an occasional hissing growl admonished us that we were in a dangerous precinct. The peons, who had now in many instances descended and joined our company, tried to point the foe's situation out, but our European eyes,[*] less keen, failed to see him. At length, after

contres is truly surprising. Yet when once these people imbibe a taste for field sports, no number of accidents, but only death, will cause them to relinquish the pursuit.

[*] The keenness of the vision of the natives is truly surprising, and often have I had game pointed out which every exertion failed to make me see.

INCAPABLE OF MISCHIEF.

moving both to the right and left, a portion of the animal's tail was plainly discerned, moving slowly but regularly to and fro, a certain indication that mischief is brewing. Not more than fifty feet intervened, and two bounds would place him in our midst. Providence, which has gifted me with more than usually sharp vision, at length helped me to distinguish a fawn-coloured patch, traversed by a dark line between the brush and gigantic-leaved grasses, and from its distance from the moving extremity of the carcase I had little doubt it must be in near proximity with a vital portion. This discovery I conveyed to my companions in a subdued whisper, and as I levelled to fire, I cautioned the others to be on the *qui vive*. Simultaneously with my report the tiger rose rampant on hind limbs, as with the intention of springing upon us; but McCarthy and Peel's quick shooting brought him down equally rapidly and as the marauder struggled upon the blood-stained soil, a few more bullets gave him the *coup de grâce*.*

Each, I believe, drew a long and thankful breath at the result; at least I know I did, for a tiger in this position, wounded and unable to make his escape, is a foe far from contemptible. On examining the carcase we found that the plucky fellow whom he had mauled spoke truly, for a deep gash was found over the exterior muscles

---

* *Dimensions of an average-sized Tiger.*—Length, including tail, 9 ft. 6 in.; height at shoulder, 3 ft. 2 in.; girth round chest, 5 ft. 6 in.; girth of arm, 2 ft. 8 in.; girth of collar, 3 ft.; length of tail, 2 ft. 9 in. Many, however, have been killed much larger. I have frequently seen hides upwards of 11 ft. The panther of India is quite as dangerous as the tiger; in size he is smaller and lighter in build, but appears to be possessed of greater activity, while his vitality is proverbial.

of the forearm that must seriously have lessened his travelling powers. Thus fell the destroyer of Peel's pointer, and many were the rejoicings and congratulations over our success. On our return to camp, while straggling behind my companions, and traversing an open meadow, I came across a wolf, and as my little Arab was fresh, and would be benefited by a gallop, I determined to try the feat of riding Mr. Lupus down. Two hundred yards was the extent of the law he had, and ere we had gone a mile, I was alongside A few strides more enabled me to send a bullet from my pistol through his valueless hide. This feat I have since performed in America, and any person well mounted can do likewise. However, I must say that the wolf of America, particularly the large grey species, is more fleet and enduring than his Asiatic brother, owing, no doubt, to the effects of climate and superiority of size.

That night was our last together, and a merry one it was; the stalwart, giant trees of the tope reverberated with the echoes of old familiar songs; the happy, reckless, joyous laugh sounded far and near, and, as is usual on such occasions, it was unanimously sung and doubtlessly recorded without dissenting voice, that all were jolly good fellows. If some travelling stranger should happen to pass this camping-ground, doubtless the *débris* of broken bottles, like tombstones, mark departed spirits.

Next morning after breakfast we broke up, never to meet again. How sad the words! As in Mrs. Hemans' 'Graves of a Household,' the majority sleep the calm, still rest of death in different scattered climes; three fell, though not with their colours round their breast, yet under the flag they had sworn to defend with life. My little Arab, if he still lives, carries a stranger, and is reined by one who probably knows not of his former prowess in the hunting-field, for before parting with him he won two races at the cantonment meeting, making your humble servant flush of rupees. But whatever prosperity fortune has or may vouchsafe me, never can I forget the picturesque, happy encampment, or the true sterling friends with whom I hunted in the Todah Valley.

CHAPTER XIV.

A FOREST SCENE.

THE diversity of climate and scenery in India is very great. Hitherto my sporting had been confined to ridable ground, but if my kind young friends will go with me, I will attempt to give them some idea of the alluvial portions of the country, where the forest grows so densely that the light of the sun is shut out, and where the fat, slimy soil gives forth vapours noxious to nearly all animals except amphibii. Such are the jungly regions formed by the delta of the Ganges —familiarly known as the Sunderbunds.

I had taken my gun and advanced into the jungle immediately after tiffin, accompanied by two natives, in order to try if we could not furnish our mess with some of the numerous variety of beautiful wild fowl that abound in such immense numbers in the various bayous which are to be found scattered throughout all the low-lying forest lands in the vicinity of large rivers. As it was far from improbable that we might come in contact with some of the *feræ naturæ*, I had chosen two of our most faithful attendants, who had previously proved themselves trustworthy when accident had placed me in a position of imminent danger. Of all the people I have met in different portions of the globe, there are none, in my opinion, for perfection of figure who equal the Bengalese—tall, slim, with good muscular development and handsome faces, the artist might find subjects for his pencil in this Eastern continent, in every way equal to the most approved torsos of Italy. Often have I watched the native women, with their scant drapery gracefully falling from one shoulder, and their lotas or water-jars balanced on their heads, going or returning from the tanks, their backs, arms, and limbs emphatically showing that nature had used her choicest moulds in their construction.

Not a breath of air was circulating; I was suffering from the intense heat, and consequently advanced with slow and exhausted steps. At last we struck a sheet of water, a narrow bayou that penetrated far into the jungle, edged on both sides by a thick growth of mangroves, leaving few spots where it was possible for a man to gain its brink without an immense amount of exertion. Near the head of the lake was an open clear space, on which lay the body of a dead buffalo, who had probably received his death-blow from the unerring bullet of some European, and had wandered away to the forest haunts of his youth to yield up his noble spirit. Although we all stood close to this ponderous carcase, an unusually large muggar, or alligator, slowly emerged from his watery retreat, and, either ignorant of our proximity or regardless of our presence, advanced upon the mountain of carrion, and commenced, with a rapacity fearfully disgusting, to satiate his noonday appetite. Around on different sides could be seen his numerous *confrères* intently watching his movements, but afraid to intrude upon his lordly presence, while vultures and adjutants swarmed on every limb, waiting for their turn to share in the offensive banquet. The solitariness and asperity of the spot, the sluggishness and murkiness of the lake, the extreme denseness of the foliage, together with the almost cavernous gloom which such a concurrence of causes produced, were seen in awful contrast with the several varieties of living objects that met the sight on entering this sequestered glade. As such scenes as this are only occasionally to be enjoyed, and that only by the sportsman, far from the haunts of man, they are doubly impressive, and leave behind them indelible impressions, which up to the latest periods of life are never forgotten. The mental associations excited by the scene before me were anything but pleasing, as we here read in one of Nature's most melancholy pages the sad lesson of animal selfishness and ferocity. In the rational creature, I fear it is the master-spring of motives, intents, and actions, and exists as strongly as it does in the irrational; in the latter, it is only the more obvious because it is the less disguised. These reflections passed rapidly through my thoughts as I gazed upon the living things which swarmed in and about the dark water, on whose banks the buffalo had breathed his last. As time elapsed, numerous and varied additions were made to the hungry assembly already collected, various beasts and birds of prey, with reptiles of the most obnoxious and horrible appearance, each hoping for the time when they should be sufficiently strong to usurp the place of honour and keep at a respectful distance the weaker claimants.

During all this time the large alligator was tearing off immense pieces of putrid carrion, and stowing them away with as much ease and gusto as a gastronome would the most tempting tit-bits. A spirit of hatred and enmity, or perhaps of tyranny and destruction, prompted me to enter the list of claimants for the spoil, not that I could make use of the booty, but perhaps to exult in the pleasure of destruction so common to man, and like the dog in the manger, refuse the food which I myself could only loathe. Towards the majority of animals I have a strong feeling of kindness, amounting to love, particularly if they be of a timid disposition, but for the bloated snake or scaly crocodile, the antipathy which is excited can only be appeased by their destruction. Giving way to these sensations, I raised my heavy rifle, glanced quick and steadily along its unerring barrels, and a dull "thud" answered as an echo to the report. The large, savage eyeball was my target, and the missive sped true to the aim. A few convulsive, spasmodic quivers were the result, and the gorged terror of the miasmatic lagoon lay helpless, in turn to become the food of those he had ruled with such tyrant sway during his lifetime. In killing most species of game, I have always felt a qualm at depriving a helpless animal of life, but on this occasion I turned from my handiwork well satisfied with my performance.

Towards night, on my return, I visited the spot, and dozens were feeding now where formerly there had only been one. The buffalo had almost totally disappeared, and a large inroad had been made upon the alligator, several of whose children and brothers, with bloody tusks, were tearing away at his vitals. As I returned towards my temporary forest bivouac, I, moralising, thought of the correctness of the proverb, "*Hodie mihi, cras tibi,*" which not inappropriately is inscribed upon the gateway to the graveyard in the Happy Valley, Hong Kong.

CHAPTER XV.

CATCHING A SHARK.

AGAIN at sea, and the blue line of coast that marks faintly the northern distance is all I expect to see of India Proper for at least some time to come.

Off to the eastward, with her sails idly flapping in the wind, lies one of the piolate brigs. Staunch crafts are they, and make as good sailors as ever trod a deck, or laid their ship to in a cyclone. All down the Bay of Bengal the weather continued fine—too fine, in fact, to suit those in a hurry. Each day, consequently, was a repetition of its predecessor; eating, sleeping, and smoking occupying the greatest portion of our time. At length the welcome cry of land was heard; the landsmen strained their eyes to see it, and wished it were closer; the sailors distinctly made it out, and wished it farther off. At length a little fun took place—fun which had the effect of sweetening some of our tempers, which were beginning to become soured.

People exhibit their true dispositions, without the

faintest attempt at disguise, when they have been a few months at sea. Often those who have borne the character of being the jolliest, kindest, and most obliging comrades turn fractious and snappish under the ordeal (a long sea-voyage), unable even to answer a civil question without a display of ill-humour.

I once sailed in a troop ship round the Cape of Good Hope. The passage was a long one, and there was more bickering and squabbling than I ever previously experienced in a similar length of time. Even the ladies, of whom we had over a dozen on board, followed the evil example of the sterner sex, and scarcely were on speaking terms with each other when the anchor was dropped in port.

Any excitement, therefore, on board ship that breaks the monotony of a sea-voyage is most acceptable.

A day or two after making the coast of Sumatra and approaching the Straits of Sunda, a shark was seen following in the wake of the troop ship. Numerous were the attempts made to capture him, but the scoundrel was too well fed or too dainty to take the most tempting bait. Fowl, turtle, pork, and beef were alternately substituted as lures, but without avail. Doubtless there were so many tit-bits falling from the ship on which Mr. Shark could regale that he did not care to lay hold of anything attached to hook or line. The majority on board, with the exception of myself, gave up the task as useless. I planned and plotted his capture, for the specimen was of a rare variety; but long I was without success. There he remained day after day, either close up to the rudder or under either of the ship's quarters. The weather was fine, the sea smooth as glass, and every movement of his fins or tail was perfectly apparent to those looking at him from the deck.

In rummaging over some old effects I found gimp and hooks, originally intended for Lough Corrib pike. I knew the tackle to be strong, and with it I resolved to make one more essay for the capture of our grim attendant.

That day I was on duty; and as our commanding officer, one of the best-hearted men breathing, but at the same time a strict disciplinarian, always insisted on the officer on duty remaining on deck during dinner, I thought that while all were below and everything quiet, the opportunity should be taken, and that the results would be more probably successful.

With a nice little piece of fat pork about the size of a walnut for bait, over went my tackle. The vessel had scarcely steerage way, and slowly I paid off line. The shark was at his accustomed place. He saw the attraction, slowly swam to it, carefully surveyed it, and again returned to his post. It was no use. Again and again it was dropped under his nose. He had seen enough, and rejected with scorn the imposition.

I had thoroughly made up my mind that all chance of success was over, and commenced in consequence throwing overboard the remainder of my bait, the first piece of which he took gingerly, the second with more avidity, and the third with considerable energy. Shakspeare's remark, that "increase of appetite doth grow with what it feeds on," was evidently being verified. I sent for a fresh supply of pork. Over a dozen morsels had been supplied to the shark, and his timidity had vanished ; for ere the ripples that succeeded the splash of their descent had enlarged to the circumference of a foot, the *bonne bouche* was seized and pouched.

Again I resorted to my line, shortening it, so that the bait alone would strike the water. Overboard it went. The savage was sold, and in a moment I had him fast. What a struggle his first effort was on finding himself hooked ! He remained on the surface, and beat the water into foam. At length, finding this mode of procedure useless, with a swirl of the tail, he went downwards almost perpendicularly, till he was lost to sight, and the strain on the line alone told that the game was still on. My tackle was too light to put a strong check on. However, I had plenty of line, so determined to play my fish in the thoroughly orthodox way. Well, I paid off to him till I had almost all my line overboard. Despair had all but seized me, for well I knew if compelled to put on a stop that the tackle must break, and my hoped-for triumph be quashed ; but in the very nick of time—not one moment too soon—the quarry turned, and I had the intense satisfaction of feeling that but for some unseen accident I should secure my prize. By this time the poop-deck was crowded. Among the officers were several fishermen. All gave advice ; but remembering the proverb of "too many cooks," I did what had previously enabled me to land many a noble salmon. At length my fish was brought alongside ; for after the run, like a coward, he gave up the battle. The first mate stood in the mizen-chains, harpoon in hand, and, as opportunity presented itself, let drive his missile with well-directed aim; but the harpoon was blunt, and glanced off, doing no other injury than instilling fresh energy into the victim. The result of this mishap was that all my labours had to be begun again, and the shark fought this second battle with greater obstinacy than the first. Again and again I gave and took in line. My foe had been too badly treated when previously alongside to be brought into the same position without resistance. At least ten minutes of this give-and-take business must have occurred, when a rope, with a noose formed by a running bowline knot, was passed down the line. With a little manœuvring it was coaxed over the shark's head; by degrees farther backwards, till the dorsal fin was reached, when a quick jerk closed the slip, and the prey was safe from escape. The line was now passed through a block, and a dozen stalwart grenadiers trolled the struggling scoundrel aloft, and ultimately dropped him on deck. The cook, a black man—all ships cooks appear to be black—stood by, chopper in hand. A grin suffused his ebony countenance; pleasure was expressed in every feature of his face; his mouth opened from ear to ear; his dusky eyes rolled about with delight; it was evident to all that he regarded the present opportunity as one for distinction; the wrigglings of the shark had scarcely ceased; forward rushed Sambo to cut off his tail. However " man proposes, God disposes." His foot slipped, and he got such a whack from the caudal appendage of the struggler as, doubtless, he still remembers well. The darkie was game, however. He made a second attempt, which was successful.

K

On opening the shark's stomach, a most extraordinary collection of articles was found—pieces of glass, cloth, a portion of a book, and several fowls' heads; the latter, no doubt, the craniums of the unfortunates who had furnished our mess with curry or spatch-cock. On measurement, this fish was eight feet long—a size attained by very few of this particular species.

The vessel on which this little episode occurred, and on which I enjoyed many happy hours, in a subsequent voyage a year or two afterwards, disappeared—probably foundered. To this day nothing has ever been heard of her.

CHAPTER XVI.

TRICKING AN ALLIGATOR.

HOW was that alligator caught? Perhaps my readers as well as the friend who asked me this question would like to know, for he was by odds the largest I have ever become on intimate terms with.

To my knowledge a more picturesque and productive island than Java does not exist, and although situated close to the equator, it is both healthy and cool. The Dutch are its possessors, and well they control and manage the natives and the productions. The Straits of Sunda form the northern boundary of this colony of Holland, and separate it from Sumatra. For ships from the westward of the Cape of Good Hope and bound farther to the east these straits are generally selected as the route to pass through the Malay Archipelago. I had come from the west: our passage had been tedious and rough, our vessel wanted provisions, water, and repairs, so at the picturesque village of Anjer, in Java, and on the Straits of Sunda, we dropped anchor and remained for some days.

Close to where we were moored was the place from whence ships' crews obtain water, a small stream emptying itself into a miniature bay. This spot had long been haunted by an immense alligator, and although innumerable devices had been practised to accomplish his capture, all had turned out unsuccessful. Scarcely a week passed that some depredation was not committed by this brute; one time a child was a victim, next a washerwoman, and so crafty had the villain become that it was almost impossible for those who from necessity frequented the stream for the purpose of washing to escape his formidable jaws.

The day previous to my arrival another victim had been added to the already formidable list, and this quiet village was in as great a state of excitement as a Hindoo hamlet would be when a man-eating tiger is known to have taken up his residence in a neighbouring ravine.

Having called upon the commandant, a splendid specimen of a Dutch naval officer, than whom no better are to be found, after the customary courtesies, I was honoured by an invitation to his table, a pleasure I was not backward to avail myself of, for I had long become disgusted with the usual ship's salt rations, and the prospect of a good feed on fresh meat, and doubtless vegetables, were temptations of no ordinary character; moreover, the society of a gentleman traveller who had probably buffeted over half the earth could not fail in assisting time to fly both rapidly and pleasantly.

A more genial host I have seldom met, or one better qualified to relate his experiences; and when the cheroots and joss stick were placed upon the table the *entente cordiale* between us was thoroughly established. I know not how many bumpers of Bordeaux had been imbibed, when the conversation gradually changed from foreign lands to field sports, and ultimately to this dreaded alligator. The next day was determined on to make another effort for his destruction; the *modus operandi* was settled, and an unfortunate cur dog was to officiate as bait. Poor bow-wow! I pitied his lot, but the necessity of the case justified the means employed.

That evening we sat late, so very late, that in preference to returning to my cabin, I accepted a shakedown, and although I was considerably startled with my first experience of the gecho* lizard, which, soon after retiring, commenced giving vent to his feelings, I slept as soundly as storm-tossed mariners usually do when first on shore, and after a long voyage they experience the comfort of clean linen and a wide bed of sufficient length to stretch their legs in.

So soundly did sleep visit me that I doubt if I ever turned in my bed till the sonorous Chinese gong of the household summoned me to breakfast, the most enjoyable of all Oriental meals. It is not necessary to discuss the merit of different curries—the one I then ate was by far superior to any I had previously enjoyed—and the mangoes, pineapples, and mangosteens that graced the table were fit delicacies for angels—the latter especially, to which I award the palm over every fruit with which I am acquainted. From the breakfast-table we

---

* The Geckolidæ or thick-tongued lizards are common to a great portion of the East. From being harmless they are much encouraged, as they are most destructive to mosquitoes and other insects.

went to the beach, and just arrived in time to see the attempt to catch Mr. Alligator from throw-off to finish.

In a *proah* was the unhappy dog, bound, not hand and foot, but as to predicament similarly situated. Attached to his side was a large shark-hook, filed at the point sharp as a needle. The commandant's appearance was the signal to commence operations, and the Malay crew were not long in gaining the centre of the estuary. With untied legs poor doggy was thrown overboard. Lustily he struck out for shore, and the boat followed at a moderate pace paying out line. The first effort was a failure: the cur gained the shore unhurt, but the cruel capturers were not satisfied; *nolens volens* he was again lugged on board and taken still farther out in the stream. A second time overboard he went with a splash. The former swim had not apparently exhausted his energies, for soon but forty or fifty yards separated him from *terra firma*. All thought the ruse had failed; public sympathy was strongly excited in the dog's behalf, a few strokes more, and his feet would touch the bottom, when, with a tremendous swirl, fifty times greater than ever fresh run salmon made at a fly, the water appeared to open, and the swimmer with a howl disappeared. The Malays well knew their work; the boat was kept stationary and line was paid out; no unnecessary hurry was exhibited, and certainly five minutes elapsed for the prowler to pouch his bait ere a pull was taken on him, and when it was made it was not of the easy description used to hook a trout, by a simple turn of the wrist—no, the slack was gently recovered, when a strike was administered that would have driven the hook through an inch plank. As luck would have it, it took effect, and the reciprocating jerks that followed were sufficient to dislocate a man's arm or overturn a canoe. Since this I have learned that the success of the project was all chance—an alligator does not, like a pike, gorge his bait, but tears it to pieces before swallowing. The boatmen, jubilant with their success, soon made for the shore, paying out only sufficient line to retain the necessary strain to keep the hook in its hold.

Dozens of volunteers were there to receive them; the struggle was long and desperate, the impaled, one moment coming to the surface and lashing the water into foam, the next submerging himself, doubtless with the intention of grappling something at the bottom to give him additional powers of resistance. However, all his strength and strategy were unavailing; with shouts and jeers he was dragged up the muddy margin, and at length secured by numerous cords wound round each limb and his powerful tail.

From the beach he was transferred alive to the commandant's garden, where he was attached to stakes, his limbs being dragged out from under him. An immense fellow he was, eighteen feet long, and more bulky than usual. However much I dislike his race and all approximate to it, I must do this one the justice to say that he remained game and indomitable to the end.

As my kind host wished to preserve the skin uninjured that it might be forwarded to the museum at Amsterdam, poison was selected as the best means of terminating the alligator's existence. A dose of strychnine, sufficiently large to have killed a regiment, was therefore administered, placed in a cavity in a bullock's heart ; but, judging from results, the intended victim had no objection to a repetition of a similar dose. At length a corporal's guard was sent for, and over a dozen shots were fired ere the enemy succumbed. After his demise I carefully inspected the carcase when it was divested of the skin ; the head was so solid and hard that, except in the region of the eye, no ordinary projectile would have done him injury ; the hide, especially along the vertebræ, was also capable of repelling a bullet from a musket, for it was not only hard as horn, but several inches thick.

While at Java, let me say that I enjoyed several days' excellent shooting. About a mile from Anjer, after passing through the cocoa-nut groves that margin the beach, commences an immense lagoon, well stocked with snipe and wild duck. Of the former the painted species will be found the most abundant ; cranes, egrets, and bitterns are also plentiful, while the neighbouring high grounds swarm with common and painted quail, and, where timber grows, with countless squirrels. In this lagoon are plenty of alligators, on the high grounds an abundance of snakes.

A native wanted my shooting companion and self to try our skill on the former, but when we were shown his ticklish canoe, in which it would be necessary for us to embark, to insure success, without further delay we declined the polite invitation. One snake that I cut in two with a charge of shot was dissimilar to any I have previously or since met with ; it was over five feet in length, and very thick in proportion ; its fangs were extremely large, the head blunt and flat ; while the colour on the back was drab, becoming gradually white as it approached the belly.

At Anjer I was first introduced to a most delicious beverage—viz., the contents of a decapitated green cocoa-nut with a proportionate mixture of old Jamaica rum. On a warm day nothing can be more delicious or more insinuating; so take warning if circumstances should place you where it can be enjoyed, for my friend who shot with me, still thirsty and desirous of imbibing more, commenced singing "We won't go home till morning" before we had got our costumes changed preparatory to sitting down to dinner. Next morning he assured me, however, that he was without a vestige of a headache.

CHAPTER XVII.

FAST ON A CORAL REEF.

READER, have you ever been, during a calm, on board a steam-ship while it threaded the intricacies of coral reefs and shoals that too frequently interrupt navigation in a landlocked tropical sea? Such was once my fate. The weather had been of that brilliant-heated nature that might have been anticipated in the month of December, when the figure that told our latitude was denoted by a unit. The day had been intensely warm, no place or position in cabin or on deck was bearable, and although an awning covered the poop, the appearance of comfort that various attitudes denoted was only an assumption; the destruction of Manilla cheroots and the consumption of cool drinks was frightfully great—both, doubtless, being considered excellent repellents of the heat emanating from a vertical sun. Not the faintest ripple that spoke of a puff of wind had darkened the water all through the day, the temperature had been stifling, overpowering; even the Lascar portion of the crew appeared to suffer under its influence, and all the ship's company who had duty to perform did it with that apathy that clearly told how little they felt like work, and how distasteful exertion was under existing circumstances. The sun, at length, disappeared beneath the horizon, amid all the glories of a tropical sunset, nor was his disappearance regarded with regret, all hoping that with darkness a mitigation of heat would take place. Nor were our hopes disappointed, for ere the last day-watch terminated, an occasional breath of air reanimated all, and gave us hopes of a speedy termination to our sufferings. Still the water looked as if oil had been poured over it, so calm and smooth was its surface; and when a glorious full moon arose, the coast of Sumatra on one side, distant about two miles, and the island of Banca on the other, faint from being farther off, were both to be seen. Who that has ever travelled through the Malay Archipelago can forget the dense tropical verdure that lines the shore of the numerous islands; the graceful palms waving in profusion to the water's edge; the rarefied clear sky and the transparent blue water!

Soon after eight bells (midnight) I went round my sentries, and finding all correct retired to my berth with the hope of sleeping. Of course, long ere this hour, lights had been extinguished, and the important ceremony of undressing was therefore being performed in the dark, when a tremendous thump, which threw me off my feet, and nearly forced me through the bulkhead, followed by a crashing noise, intermingled with abundant orders, and exclamations from the officer and watch on deck, announced that the ship was either on a reef or on shore. Catching up those articles of apparel which came first, in a moment I was on deck; orders were being issued for the engines to be reversed; up each hatchway swarmed my soldiers. With quickest steps the crew rushed about performing various services, while the captain, in a state of frenzy, appeared ubiquitous, and our noble vessel, instead of being on a horizontal keel, had her stem stuck up in the air as if star-gazing, while her stern was correspondingly depressed. One glance told the story, we were on a coral reef, hard and fast, and our prospect of getting off uninjured entirely depended on the sea remaining calm. Without confusion the soldiers fell into their respective places, ready to act in whatever capacity their services might be required—such is the result of discipline and education! For coolness and courage in the hour of danger, I will back my countrymen by long odds against any others in the world. Fortunately the steam-ship had only been going at half-speed, or our situation would have been dangerous in the extreme—as it was, our grip of the reef was so strong that the reversed engines under a full head of steam failed to release us. Shifting cargo, so as to change the trim of the ship, was next adopted, but without avail; anchors afterwards were got out astern, and the capstans manned, but with no better success. If the long-wished-for breeze were now to spring up, in an hour or two our temporary home would be in pieces. With reluctance, orders were given for the boats to be prepared for sea. Stewards hurried about looking after stores and water-breakers, while the junior officers examined oars and thole-pins.

Of course, as long as the vessel remained together, we intended sticking to her, but in case of symptoms of dissolution then a boat excursion of several hundred miles was our only alternative. No one with a particle of feeling could help commiserating our captain; he was a young man, this was his first voyage in command, and he loved his ship as all good sailors love a noble vessel. Moreover, it was not only the loss of the craft and all his personal effects which he would sustain, but his reputation as a navigator and skill as a seaman would suffer a blemish that perhaps years of future good conduct would not erase. So far, we have only been looking at the dark side; however, it is well to be prepared for contingencies, although on this occasion they did not occur. The traffic on deck was observed to impart a tremulous motion to the ship—could this but be increased, her hold of the coral reef would be lessened. So the captain thought, and so did others. "Come, my lads," I called to my men, "fall in along the bulwarks." With alacrity the soldiers obeyed "Fours deep—close on your centre—quick march—double," immediately followed; and thus forming the men into a solid mass, they were trotted across decks, the engines at the same time being reversed under a full head of steam. "By Jove!—she moves!—keep up the tramp!—well done," for slowly at first, but with gradually increasing pace, the ship commenced to slide; when gaining velocity, backwards she shot afloat upon her watery home. Some anxiety was felt as to the injury she might have suffered, but the carpenter put this at rest, for having sounded the well, he reported that no leak had been sprung. The coral reef on which we had struck was not marked on our charts; in appearance it resembled a huge mushroom, with the upper portion within a few feet of the surface of the water. With great caution and under half-speed we proceeded to Singapore, on the Straits of Malacca, where divers were employed to inspect the ship's bottom; all the injury she had suffered was the loss of a few sheets of copper and the carrying away of a portion of her fore foot. But the examination and the performing of some necessary repairs caused a delay of several days, the very thing I desired most, for on my previous visit to this beautiful settlement my stay was so contracted that I had not half the time I wished to visit the surrounding neighbourhood, so productive of food for the naturalist.

CHAPTER XVIII.

A BATTLE IN A BILLIARD-ROOM.

WHO that has visited Singapore can forget the pretty town, the magnificent tropical vegetation, the numerous islands, and shipping of every rig and nationality? The costumes here to an European's eye are as quaint as they are numerous. The Tartar and Chinaman, Hindoo and Parsee, Malay and Arab, are all to be found, making as great a Babel of the market-place as that of Gibraltar on a Sunday morning. But although these sights made a strong impression, a little episode in which I played the part of principal left an impression on my mind never to be forgotten.

I had arrived at Singapore from Hong Kong in charge of invalids, the ship was ordered to the new harbour to take in coals, and I found myself with an abundance of spare time and disposition for wandering. At last the day for our departure approached. I bade adieu to new acquaintances, and I had arranged with an old and tried friend to meet for perhaps the last time and spend our final evening together at the billiard-rooms attached to the Esperanza Hotel. At half-past ten I dropped into the place of rendezvous; the room was unoccupied, except by a Chinese marker and a stranger, who lay apparently asleep on one of the benches. Now, this billiard-room was an immense place. I think it contained eight or ten tables, with abundance of space for several others. On entering, the marker was covering up his table, but on stating my desire to play, and thus keep the place open till my friend arrived, the cover was removed and a game commenced.

My boyish days, except when at school, were all spent in a barrack. Was it, then, to be wondered at that single-stick and foils had become amusements at which I was an adept? In fact, few could excel me in either of these pastimes; and conscious of my science, I took pleasure in practice whenever opportunity occurred. Well that it was so, for but for that skill I should not now be alive to narrate what I am about to tell.

Our game proceeded without interruption till the Chinaman had scored forty-seven and I forty-eight. Then my antagonist marked three more and proclaimed himself victor. Previous to this I had been in the habit of playing a game of sixty-three points, and on stating so, as well as my belief that, if the other thirteen points were added, I could with facility win, the marker was satisfied to continue the game, provided I agreed to pay whether I lost or won.

But this arrangement was not permitted to be put in execution, for the unknown who slept upon the bench sprang from his seat, and, rushing towards me, reviled me in the grossest language as a swindler and a cheat. It was no use trying to play, for, without cessation, an entire vocabulary of vituperation was hurled at me.

Flesh and blood may be over-taxed, and at length my patience gave way, and my tongue became loosed. "You black son of a sea-cook, sit down, or, if you interrupt me again, I'll——!" &c., &c., I exclaimed. "What you call me—a black son of a sea-cook? You repeat it, if you dare." I did so. While I was repeating my words, he aimed a blow at me, and I parried. Again he struck at me, with no better results. A third time the attempt was made, and, by way of change, I added to the programme by making a feint with my left hand, knocking my adversary down with the right. So far I had avoided a contest; now I was in for it. Soon the foe was on his feet; and twice more I brought him, by a straight hit from the elbow, to his knees. Finding that the game was decidedly adverse to him, he gathered himself together, rushed to the door of the room, and sounded a war-whoop. But a few moments elapsed before it was answered, and in rushed four Chinamen. They all made for the cue-rack, and each grasped a weapon. I saw from their manner that mischief was intended, so breaking the cue I had played with through the centre, and doubling my shell-jacket around my arm, I retreated into a corner, for my foes were between me and the door.

From the manner and appearance of my antagonists, I felt that life depended upon my skill and pluck. Who under such circumstances would not be a craven to succumb as long as he had a breath left in him or power to

L

raise his hand? Even a cornered rat will fight. So, little credit is due to me for making as long and desperate a resistance as was in my power. With my back in a corner I quietly waited the issue. With a rush my foes came at me, but my determined appearance and position caused them momentarily to recoil. Chinamen are cowards, the veriest of curs. I know them well, and have always found them so. The prospect of resistance, even with such tremendous odds in their favour, would have caused them to decline the contest; but the villain, he whom I struck, urged them on, and fierce and fast became the battle. Their numbers and the length of their weapons impeded them. The position I had selected harassed and crowded the assailants together, and for some minutes I successfully parried all blows, returning the compliment when opportunity offered. How long this lasted it would be impossible to say correctly. At length the violence of my exertions commenced to tell. Already my left arm, which I had used as a guard, dropped helpless by my side; blood from several cuts coursed down my face, and once I had been brought to my knees. In a moment I decided to try and fight my way through them. An opportunity immediately afterwards occurred. The instigator was directly in my front, concentrating all his strength for a blow. I received it on my broken cue, so close to his hand that the force of the stroke disarmed him. With the velocity of thought I recovered and struck him at the base of the ear, felling him to the ground. With a rush I sprang over his prostrate figure; few of the blows aimed at me took effect, and at the greatest speed I could summon I rushed out of the building. My speed of foot carried me away from the ruck. Only one was able to keep pace; and as I passed down the covered way which connected the billiard-room with the hotel, I watched my chance, wheeled sharply round and gave him a blow across the cranium which doubtless to this day has left a mark. In the hotel all had retired to rest; doors and windows stood open, after the manner of the East; so, seeing no one, I passed on and made for the Masonic Arms, a smaller house, where two friends were staying —the one a surgeon in our army, the other a lieutenant of a Bengal regiment of cavalry. On reaching this establishment my strength failed me, and the landlord (once boatswain to Rajah Brooke's yacht) assisted me to a chair. Soon the surgeon came to me, a glass of brandy and water recalled my scattered senses, and eight or ten stitches in different portions of my head drew the various contused and broken wounds together. When I narrated to L. what had taken place, he advised me to go to the magistrate, and volunteered to accompany me. He was found at his post of duty, and within a few minutes a posse of police, with the gallant surgeon and myself at their head, might have been seen returning to the battle-field. You must not imagine that I walked. No, I was far too weak for that; but a comfortable Chinese chair, borne by two coolies, performed the duty of conveyance. For some time we unsuccessfully searched for the would-be assassins. At length the whole party were captured in an outhouse, firmly secured, and marched off to the lock-up. Next morning I had to attend the police court. When the prisoners

L 2

were produced, none but those who witnessed their appearance could possibly believe that one man could inflict such injury on six. The instigator (a South American Spaniard) had a fearful wound; the others were all more or less contused or cut; and when, unwashed and dirty, they were ranged in the dock, they almost elicited pity, from their woe-begone and haggard appearance. The sentences passed upon them all were adequate to their deserts, and the billiard-room was temporarily closed.

That the above is true there are abundant witnesses to prove. I do not tell it as a proof of my courage, but as a reason that all should study the art of self-defence, for, if a traveller, you know not what hour your skill may be called upon to save your life. In the neighbourhood where this took place, a few weeks before, a merchant skipper was found murdered. The gang who assailed me were strongly suspected to be the perpetrators.

CHAPTER XIX.

CHASED BY A BUFFALO.

NOT more than ten miles from Hong Kong, inland, the sportsman reaches the margin of Meer's Bay. From the garrison, looking across to Kowloon, nothing but the straggling city of that name, backed by ranges of sterile sun-burnt hills, greets the vision; but ascend to the summit of these ridges—no easy matter—and the sterility has fled, the placid waters of Meer's Bay lie off, some miles beneath, scattered villages dot its margin, while numerous woods, instead of stunted brush, are to be seen on every side. The repose and picturesqueness of this scene has often delighted me, for the water is blue and pellucid, the vegetation brilliantly green, and the inhabitants' domiciles, at a distance, appear white as snow—a pleasant contrast to the surrounding foliage. From this bay branch off in every direction numerous valleys, many of which are cultivated, rice being predominant in the lower ground, tea and pineapples in the more elevated situations.

I had succeeded in obtaining leave of absence for a week, and so early a start had companions and self made on the occasion referred to that ere the sun had risen we—for our party consisted of four sportsmen and numerous coolies—were over the Kowloon ridge, and as the day advanced and the mists gradually evaporated, we looked forward with much pleasure to our holiday and prospects of amusement.

To describe my friends is necessary. Two were commonplace mortals, at least their arms and legs were all in the right places, but the third—well, he was not deformed, but he was the shortest and stoutest man that ever gloried in the use of dog and gun, and he *did* glory in it. It mattered not how hot the day was, how steep the hills, how boggy the paddy fields, how stiff the brush —on, on, he would toil, from morning to night; and neither did it signify how many birds he missed—and they were numerous—"*en avant*" was always his watchword, and the equanimity of his temper ever remained up to this excursion undisturbed. He was, in fact, a jolly companion, a thoroughly good fellow, the life and soul of every party he attached himself to, and, moreover, a man who had seen much of the world and profited by it, one whom once known never could be forgotten. But he was a foreigner, and, like foreigners, had some ideas which did not exactly tally with our own. Among others was his love of display; coats with innumerable pockets, powder-flasks and shot-pouches of the newest and most awkward shapes, suspended by cords of green and red, terminating with tassels, hung about his fully-developed person, while drinking-flasks, game-bags, and other additions dangled wherever they could be stuck.

It mattered not how hot it was, and Southern China is not proverbial for coolness, my stout friend would sooner part with his life, suffer a stroke of *coup de soleil*, than dismantle himself of one of these playthings. Often have I seen him toiling up the side of a hill, every pore of his skin in active operation, with his collar closed to the throat, while we were dressed in the lightest garb, unbuttoned at every possible point where decency would permit, or the retention of our clothes on our backs allow.

To this day I believe he considered that game demanded this honour and self-sacrifice, that the loss of comfort was necessary to success, and that unless he retained all these cockneyfied addenda, he would be unable to hold his gun straight or pull his triggers.

Well, the ground we had to get over was traversed, and from our noonday halting-place we determined to commence operations by beating a sparse cover, known invariably to contain pheasants. For over an hour we were unsuccessful; a few birds were seen, but were so wild that the greatest advocate for long shots would not have dreamt of throwing away a charge after them; however, in a pineapple grove at the top of a valley, better results were anticipated. In this we were not mistaken, for the moment we reached its margin, not less than a dozen birds flushed, each taking wing at the same moment (in fact, similar to a covey of partridge early in the season), out of whose ranks we tumbled over three; the remainder were marked down on the slope of a hill, a few hundred yards distant, where were feeding half a dozen water buffaloes, the beast of draft always here employed for ploughing heavy, wet rice lands.

The dogs were whistled up by our stout friend, to whom they belonged ; the coolies were called from cover, and with confident hopes of success we started for the marked birds. Off went the brace of pointers through the long, coarse grass, when their master waved his hand as a signal that their services were again required. Forward we advanced in line ; back and forth the canines quartered their ground, with nothing to interrupt their progress, except here and there an occasional dwarf pine. Now these trees were not above fifty feet high, very sparse of limbs except at the summit, and the interval between each tree was probably over one hundred yards. In skirmishing order we advanced. By this time the dogs had commenced to wind their game, when the confounded buffaloes closed on their centre, tossed up their heads, sniffed the air, and pawed the ground. Such conduct was not to be mistaken ; their intentions were evidently hostile, nor were we long kept in suspense of their *modus operandi*. The patriarch of the drove, a giant old bull, stepped to the front, glorious in his hairless, mud-baked coat, and advanced with measured steps upon the now standing pointers. For their safety we had no fear, for the water-buffalo is not fleet, and very awkward, but that the brutes would flush our game ere we were within shooting distance amounted to a certainty. It was no use hallooing or gesticulating ; onward came the foe, the dogs looked uneasy, commenced to waver, and ultimately, as the pheasants flushed, completely wheeled to the right-about and fled, followed by the bull at his best pace. For some minutes our shooting assistants satisfied themselves by keeping sufficiently in advance of their

A RUDE INTRUSION.

pursuer to avoid being run over, but their patience became so thoroughly taxed that as a last resource they sought their jolly stout owner for protection. With despair written on our friend's countenance, he exhausted his vocabulary of terms to drive his dogs from him; all was of no avail, and worse than that, the huge, awkward buffalo changed from the former objects of its ire and came straight at their owner. For a moment my friend hesitated. Only for a moment did he appear in doubt, when, suddenly spinning round, he bolted down hill for the nearest tree with all the velocity and impetus that his legs and weight could command, closely followed by his cloven-footed foe.

Never to this day have I seen a more ludicrous scene; if I should live to the age of Methuselah never shall I again; and the rest of our party were possessed of the same opinion. I do not believe, even supposing the situation had been one of most imminent danger, either of us, from the immoderate fit of laughter with which we were seized, could have gone to his assistance. But such a race between two welter weights could not last long; the tree was reached, and clasping its stem with his right hand, our friend drew himself round and behind it with the false hope that the pursuer would pass onwards. Mr. Buffalo, it is true, overshot his mark, and had to go some distance before he could pull up, but he was not thus to be cheated, so came back to the pursuit with more measured and cautious steps; for almost a minute each surveyed the other—ten yards did not intervene between them—first from one side of the tree, then from the other, a stare was given, when again down went the bull's head, and with tail straight on end, he re-dashed at his intended victim; fast and furious became the strife, round and round the tree our friend most agilely skipped, while the bull, unwieldy from his great length, was frequently nearly overrun by our stout but active companion. Half a dozen, possibly more, evolutions of this rotary description were accomplished, when, as if by mutual consent, both called a halt, perfectly blown from the violence of the exercise. Still our friend had not lost his voice: between every gasp for air he swore vociferously, first at the bull, then at the dogs, and lastly at our unfeeling selves for not coming to his aid. But he had to be careful; the eyes of the pursuer were still upon him; time was again about to be called as up, and the pursued had better retain his breath rather than waste it in anathemas. Again the foe's head was lowered, again the demon of destruction took possession of him, and the activity of our now profusely warm friend was put to a further ordeal. Fancy any one chased round a tree by an ordinary cow—if the pursued was not in imminent danger, the scene would be ludicrous; but the two principals, as on this occasion, were remarkable for their unwieldiness and excessively low-comedy appearance; surely, therefore, forgiveness can be found for our apparent want of feeling for indulging in laughter. The spinning round a second time ceased, each surveyed the other with increasing hate, while want of breath from fatigue was apparent. The tactics now were altered: evidently the bull had projected a deep plot of vengeance, but our companion was about to practise a deeper; each looked at the other from either side of the tree, a kind of bo-peep amusement undertaken to take the other at a disadvantage. This halt restored my friend's exhausted wind, and with its return his tongue was again loosened, nor was his vocabulary more choice, only seasoned with an occasional German interjection to make up for deficiencies in the English language. The *finale*, however, was now at hand. The previously unused gun, which had been retained in his left hand apparently forgotten, was called on for aid; an opportunity to use it as desired presented itself, and at less than ten yards the centre of the foe's tail was made the target. The aim was just such as was required, the caudal appendage was nearly severed, and the bull, thoroughly discomfited, took to his heels and fled, bellowing with pain and wrath, down the face of the hill, as quick as his short club-looking legs could go, followed by both dogs, now giving tongue in pursuit like a brace of beagles. The wind-up was as ludicrous as the episode, and, rolling in the grass, all three of us only laughed the louder as our friend joined us and hurled at our devoted heads every imprecation, in Dutch and English, known to him. Shoot with us, or be our companion again he never would, so indignant and sulky he left for our place of rendezvous. But at night, when we rejoined him with a tolerably large bag, over a glass of generous wine, his wrath became appeased to such an extent that his jolly laugh might have been heard the longest and loudest at the ridiculous appearance he must have cut, and the amusement he afforded his friends.

Strange to say, ere we sat down to dinner, an old

Chinese woman, leading the identical bull, now thoroughly submissive and crestfallen, visited our quarters, and importuned a *cumshaw* for the injury her brute had suffered. This was really adding insult to injury, and I almost expected to see our jolly friend have a fit of apoplexy, so great was his wrath and indignation at such a preposterous demand upon his purse.

In the Happy Valley at Hong Kong now sleeps the subject of this episode, among hundreds of Europeans, all premature victims to the treachery of a Southern Chinese climate. May the sod lie lightly on them all! for, as a rule, better and more hospitable people than the merchants of this distant colony are nowhere to be found.

CHAPTER XX.

AMONG CHINESE PIRATES.

ON the seaboard side of the island of Hong Kong is situated a village of considerable magnitude, called by the English, Stanley, by the Chinese, Chuck-choo. Close by, on an eminence overlooking the place, is a barrack, more intended for a sanitarium than a stronghold. Victoria, the capital, it is true, is not possessed of much attraction, but life at Stanley was complete isolation—the majority of officers who had been stationed there had either become drunkards or gamblers, or, not unfrequently, prematurely went to an early grave.

Well, what do you suppose were my feelings as, one evening, while dressing for mess, the orderly corporal of my company shoved the order-book in my hand, in which I saw myself detailed to proceed on the morrow to take command of this wretched place? Disgust in the most superlative sense.

Soon I was *en route*. The sail round the south side of the island of Hong Kong is very pretty; the hills certainly are sterile, but their outlines are bold and grand, while the water, for clearness and brilliancy of colouring, can most favourably compare with the ever-lauded Mediterranean. About three hours' voyage landed me at my destination, where I was greeted by my predecessor and the temporarily attached assistant surgeon. Let me describe the latter. He was about six feet four in height, with the frame of a Hercules and an eye dark as the raven's wing, flashing with courage and intelligence whenever he spoke. A finer or nobler specimen of a Highlander I never saw; a more true, brave, and generous-hearted friend I never met. I became an inmate of his bungalow till my own was put in order, and the first night, as we discussed our late dinner, I found there was a bond of sympathy between us that was calculated to ripen into a lasting friendship. What was that bond? you will ask. Why, we were both ardently devoted to the sports of the field and the use of the gentle, delicate fly-rod. For a couple of weeks time sped on rapid wing; each had so much to tell of his favourite pursuit that night after night, aye, well on into the wee sma' hours, we would sit on the bungalow verandah in our loblolly chairs, encased in panjamas, smoking cheroots and sipping weak brandy-pawnee, spinning or listening to each other's yarns.

Such was our occupation, the midnight relief had just marched past, and the cheery notes of the distant sentries were sounding the musical chant of "All's well," when B. turned abruptly to me with the enquiry, "Have you ever been to Lemma Island?" On answering in the negative, he continued, "Then there we will go to-morrow, if the weather is favourable, for though it's a long pull from here, the trip is worth the trouble, for I can show you a small snipe marsh where I have twice obtained four or five couple of long-bills." A bargain was struck on the spot. A day's change, at least, was a treat, and although a general order existed that both should not leave the detachment together, we laughed at the distant prospect of court-martials, and determined with one accord to accept all risks.

After discussing our chutney and curried prawns at the morrow's breakfast, the fast boat was announced as waiting. So, whistling my dear and ever-true pointer Sancho to my heels—B. armed with a shot-gun, I with a revolver, which I carried merely for protection, for we had agreed to take shot about—we hastened down to the place of embarkation.

From Stanley, Lemma Island could distinctly be seen : it lay about eight miles off, almost directly to the southward. Its general appearance is less rugged than Hong Kong, while its length is about seven miles. After a sail of three hours, the keel of our boat grated on the desired landing-place, and as we disembarked, instructions were given to the crew to proceed along the shore to a known inlet, where we would join them before sunset. As we started inland, the boat pushed off; so, for a time at least, we were separated from the rest of the world.

The sun that day was not overpoweringly hot ; a cool, strong breeze played over our faces as we breasted the opposing hill-side. Sancho, old pet, ranged far and wide, hoping that his previous experience would assist him to find a point. Up higher, higher, we ascend. Sancho finds no game, and we at length reach the summit. From here we have a grand view. Stanley, with its snow-white barrack buildings, looked no larger than a flock of scattered sheep on a hill-side. Away to the eastward was a square-rigged clipper ship on her homeward voyage, freighted with the wealth of the Celestial Empire. Think how many perils she has to encounter ere again she floats in the waters that gird her ocean birth-place! To the westward opens Hong Kong harbour. Half a dozen American and European ships can be seen, while the interval between them is crowded with every description and size of Chinese shore-boat. On turning to the other side, looking down the declivity opposite to which we had ascended, a few hundred feet beneath where we stood, lay nestled in the hills one of the pleasantest, cleanest Chinese villages, partially hidden by noble banyan trees, it has ever been my lot to look at. But that the climate is unhealthy, it would be an admirable place to which a man, regardless of amassing wealth and gaining reputation, might retire, with, perhaps, some fair being for companion. By the village, through the fields, we tramped, over hills, down ravines, till at length we reached the snipe-ground B. had mentioned. It was a hollow, between hills, sixty acres or so in extent, the greater portion of which was cultivated with rice; a part, however, was even too wet for that water-loving cereal. In the tilled and unreclaimed land we found birds; and when we rested, after an hour's work, we had seven brace of snipe and a pair of teal. Satisfied —yes, deeming ourselves well rewarded—we turned our faces towards the place of rendezvous, little doubting we should find the boat ready to receive her freight. As we descended towards the sea, a glorious Oriental sunset greeted us, and we both halted to see old Sol retire to rest behind the mighty ocean, attended by legions of clouds decked in the most refulgent coloured armour.

But time hurries on apace, night quickly follows sunset in tropical climates, and nearly a mile intervened between us and the boat. Both of us were youthful and active, and less than fifteen minutes placed us upon the shingle beach of our rendezvous. But where is the boat? Surely some mistake has taken place. The scoundrelly crew cannot have left without us. "Confound them!" "They deserve to have their heads punched!" were the ejaculations that fell from our lips. But talking was but a waste of time. Let us decide what is to be done, and let us do it quickly. In a minute our determination was that each should go along the coast in opposite directions, as, possibly, the boat might have come a less distance or gone farther. If either should find the boat, he was to return to his companion, keeping close in shore; but if unsuccessful after searching for two miles, each was to turn to the right-about, and meet where we then were about to part.

B., whistling "Bonnie Dundee," with his gun on his shoulder, took the western route; I, with Sancho at my heels, the eastern. Darkness had now dropped her sable mantle over the landscape, and many were the falls and bruises that I got as I threaded my intricate way through the almost insurmountable boulders that lay along the beach. I knew that the night was not going to be dark, because the moon rose early. Still, I wished most cordially that it rose earlier. I went through a mile of most fatiguing clambering till at length I found myself in such a *cul de sac* that a retrograde movement was absolutely necessary. To avoid a repetition of such accidents, I made a *détour* inland. As soon as I reached soil, I found walking much more favourable, for there was nothing to oppose my progress but a sparse covering of brush. But if the change was agreeable to me, it appeared quite the reverse to my dog. Occasionally he would go before me a few paces and return growling, showing every indication of anger. This conduct of Sancho's struck me as strange, indeed more than strange, indicative of trouble, for, poor old veteran, his knowledge of life had long taught him not to proclaim a false alarm. Still I saw nothing, but for the sake of caution I determined to return to the boulder-covered beach. In carrying out this decision, I turned suddenly round, and behind me, just showing over the rise in the land I had quitted, appeared the figures of several Chinamen. (I may as well tell my readers that this was in the year 1857, at a time when a price was paid for every European's head.) At once I knew that I was followed, and that with no amiable intention. Drawing my revolver from my belt and cocking it, I resolved to pursue my way, and only use my weapon if compelled to do so. I made, however, for the shore, not that it offered greater security, but intuition told me that from the sea alone help could be expected. Fain would I have turned, but I felt I had a duty to perform, and do it I would. The boulders again impeded my progress, and the rising tide caused my steps to be necessarily nearer the bluffs that descended to the beach.

After such a warning as I had received, of course I kept my eyes about me, and instead of two or three assailants I became convinced that there were at least a dozen. Their numbers made them brave, and no longer was any great amount of strategy practised to prevent their presence being known. I had almost made up my mind to place my back against a rock and fight it out, for I felt I had been headed off from further progress, when a boat shot round a point not fifty yards off. B. was in her, and, rushing through the surf and water waist-deep, I clambered on board. To explain my escape to him at that moment was unnecessary, for my pursuers, baulked in what they had considered a certain prize, lost their prudence, and, yelling, rushed upon the beach. A couple of gingalls which they carried sent their messengers whistling by us, and thus gave us fair grounds for retaliation.

B. stood up in the stern sheets ; not thirty yards from us stood conspicuous the largest of our assailants. Quickly B.'s gun was pitched to his shoulder, and with the report arose a most unearthly yell. Never have I heard a more frightful cry from those who have fallen beside me in the battle-field, or from the raving madman confined in a strait-jacket. B.'s gun was loaded with one of Eley's heavy-shot wire-cartridges.

In a few hours we reached the detachment, and just as we were about to land, I attempted to fire my revolver. Every barrel missed.

CHAPTER XXI.

SHOOTING NEAR HONG KONG.

IN speaking of Hong Kong, the uninitiated are apt to think that it is the last place in the world which choice would lead one to visit, but when you have traversed that mountainous and picturesque island, wandered through its numerous valleys, rested from the noonday sun in some of its innumerable villages, or drank the cool waters that trickle down its many rugged ravines, more especially if in the society of some of its merchant princes, whose wealth is unbounded and good-fellowship beyond comparison, I must be a false prophet indeed, or else you will most assuredly, in after years, look back with delight and satisfaction to the period you spent upon the Chinese coast.

From my youth upwards I have always kept a diary, as I should recommend all sportsmen to do, and when I take a cast back through musty and soiled pages, I find that my double-barrels did as much good and constant work when living on the confines of the Celestial

Empire, as they have executed before or after in the many climes and distant lands it has been my lot to visit.

All may not have the same opportunities as I had, for I, shortly after arrival, made the acquaintance of a thorough sportsman and kind-hearted, worthy gentleman, who kept an excellent kennel of both pointers and setters, and who kindly took me by the hand, and as chaperon introduced me to all the best localities for game, which he had found out through his own indefatigable exertions and love of adventure, during a long residence in this colony. I should have some hesitation in pointing out these hunting-grounds, for fear my worthy friend should object to the world being informed of the result of his labours; but, alas! he now sleeps peacefully in the Happy Valley, where neither dog nor gun can disturb him, warmly remembered by all who knew him, and much regretted by every one who had the honour of calling him friend. No true man or sportsman should pass his last resting-place without dropping a tear; and often have I regretted that circumstances have not carried me back to that far Eastern land, that I might pay this rightful tribute to the kindest friend, the most unselfish man, I ever met. If this introduction be deemed irrelevant, I warn my readers that I make this rhapsody the penalty for which I give my experience.

Early one bright November morning I sailed with three companions from Hong Kong harbour, on board the good fast boat 'Pat-wan.' My esteemed friend, D., was one of my associates. The others were both merchants from Canton, keen sportsmen and good fellows. A fresh, fair wind was blowing as we got under weigh, and as the large matting-sails bellied out to the wind, our craft cleft the water like a thing of life. I doubt much if there is a more secure or beautiful harbour than the one through which we were now running, nor can a greater or more numerous variety of all kinds of boats and shipping, whether European or Asiatic, be seen anywhere else. The powerful steamship, strong as timber and iron can make it, capable of encountering the much-dreaded typhoon; the graceful snake-like clipper; the heavy, lumbering, native-built East Indiaman; the opium schooner, model of fleetness and symmetry; the Shantung junk, the piratical and smuggling fast boat—all lay in one heterogeneous mass, with a perfect mosquito fleet of man-of-war's boats, flower boats, sampans, merchants' and captains' gigs, threading the intricate paths of open water left between the larger and markedly dissimilar crafts. The flag of England may predominate, but the stars and stripes, tricolour, flaunting yellow ensign of Spain, with the representative emblem of every nationality in the world, can here be found, flying at the peaks of trading vessels, for the owners of these crafts are all intent on money-making, and ready to charter to any nationality to carry tea, silk, and opium, or sometimes even do a little piratical business, if nothing else offers.

As we cleared the labyrinth of shipping, our stem was pointed for the Capsheemoon Pass, a distance of about six miles, and gallantly did we advance; but even after leaving the roadstead, our way was not uninterrupted.

First we steered through a fleet of fishing-boats; next a crowd of merchant junks, heavily freighted with the wealth of this Eastern clime, or some rapid steamboat or mandarin snake boat shoots past—all on a visit to the European emporium. What between luffing and running off our course to avoid collisions, more than an hour elapsed before we got through the passage, when, from the effect of the high lands shutting out the regular course of the wind, it was necessary to make several tacks to get a good offing for the place we intended to run to. Castle Peak Bay was our destination, and so, holding old Lin Ting on the south, we gallantly ran down for our anchoring ground. As it was only midday when we reached our journey's end, it was universally agreed that tiffin should be served before we commenced operations. The word of command was rapidly passed forward, and almost as quickly was served under the awning upon the flush deck one of those sumptuous meals for which the Orient is justly celebrated. Curry, that standing and incomparable dish; pillaw, cold meats, *pâte de foie gras*, &c. &c. forming no inconsiderable portion; and if our provender was good, no less were the liquids—ruby claret, sparkling Moselle and old Otard or United Vineyards' brandy, were in profusion. However, one drink stood paramount, and I can confidently recommend it as worthy of the votaries of Diana, viz. Moselle and soda-water. We all thought so, and many were the pear-shaped gentry that disgorged their effervescing contents to gratify our fastidious tastes. After feeling the inward man refreshed, we disembarked, and soon stood on *terra firma*, longing to commence the anticipated sport. Doe and Die, a setter and pointer, were selected for our *début*, and Sancho, a young liver-coloured pointer, a present from my friend, I determined to take, for the benefit he would receive from the example of his well-broken companions. The ground we were about to shoot over was undulating and grassy, there being no high land in the immediate vicinity, save the old Peak, from which the place takes its name. A good deal of the vicinity had been previously cultivated, but from unproductiveness, or other causes, was now neglected; still, the diminutive stone fences which characterise this country remained, and the intricate covering of briars and creepers, which almost hid them from view, was found a frequent shelter and resting-place of our quarry. Among the varieties of game which we expected to find were the lordly pheasant, refulgent in gorgeous plumage. He is indigenous to this locality, where he grows to a much greater size than I have ever seen him elsewhere, weighing frequently four pounds and a half, and sometimes even more. I killed a cock in the Shangmoon Valley, not over ten miles from our present beat, which handsomely turned down the scale at five and a half. Still, these birds are not very abundant here, this locality being scarcely far enough inland, where the covers are more extensive and better suited for their propagation. Frankolin, however, are here tolerably numerous, few days passing without a dozen or more falling to the sportsman's aim. They are larger than the partridge of England, lie remarkably close, and, when flushed, beat all the game birds put together in the velocity of their flight. To be successful, you must shoot quick, and cover them well, as they will carry off as much lead as a wild goose. Then the quail—the little migratory darlings—if you only chance to hit the time of their arrival, they will give you as much popping to do as can be stood up to. In Malta, on the coast of Spain, and among the Greek islands, I have enjoyed some splendid sport with them, and made wondrous bags, but here in Southern China they are ten to one in comparison of numbers. Don't be impatient. I have not completed my list. Snipe—the idol of the shooter—also abound. Can any one tell to what land the bird is a stranger? Here there are two species—the common bird, so numerous in Ireland, and the painted species, larger than the former, more beautiful in plumage, but lacking the velocity of flight; and last, though not least, the delicacy of flavour after passing through the cook's hands. Then as to the web-footed gentry, their name is legion, and their varieties are without number. Pelicans, geese, mallard, widgeon, and teal, being frequently seen in such hordes that the water is obscured. If you imagine that I am romancing, you have but in the winter to take a trip up the Broadway running from the back of Macao to Canton. Defer your opinion till then, and I fear not the result. There is but one place where such a sight can be seen, as well as in China, and if you have time and means, place yourself upon the margin of any of the numerous sloughs in the western prairies of America, a little after sunset, late in autumn, when the weather from appearances promises a rapid approach of winter, and I presume to predict, if you should live to the age of Methuselah, and have true sporting proclivities, the sight you will then witness never can be forgotten. But to return to the land of small-footed women and tails; seldom, if you go sufficiently inland, will a day pass without seeing deer, and probably getting a shot at them; even on the island of Hong Kong a number are to be found. Some of my regiment, on more than one occasion, brought them to bag in the woods that encircle the Happy Valley, where they used frequently to hunt them with a pack of dwarf beagles. Another species, larger and scarcer, the Formosan deer, is also to be found; on the mainland it resembles our fallow deer in size, make, and colour. I only once had the fortune to kill one, and it was deemed quite an exploit. It happened in this wise: I was shooting pheasants in the upper portion of Shangmoon Valley, and my luck had been anything but gratifying; the heat was oppressive, from the circulation of the air being shut out by the numerous mountain ridges, and I had begun to fabricate excuses for discontinuing my unprofitable business, consoling myself with the idea that I could make up in the afternoon for the lost morning hour. When about to retrace my steps to the Joss house, where I had left my attendants, with instructions to prepare breakfast, I observed a crowd of Celestials, with banners flying and other insignia of pomp, descending an opposite declivity. From what I knew of the manners of this strange people, I concluded it was a funeral party, and silently watched their grotesque proceedings. On they advanced, making the rocks reverberate with their disjointed howlings; a deer was unkennelled by their approach, and made direct for my resting-place. Beneath was a stream which he had to ford if he continued his course. When the antlered gentleman reached the water, he stood and gazed with apparent curiosity at the mixed crowd of ragamuffins who had ousted him from his lair. Some minutes elapsed ere he made up his mind to wet his feet, which delay I turned to account by slipping an Eley green cartridge into each barrel, having taken care to avail myself of the friendly shelter of some brush. As the mob advanced closer upon him, deeming his safety imperilled, he crossed the brook and offered me as beautiful a side shot, at thirty-five yards, as the most fastidious could desire. Simultaneously with the report his graceful form bit the dust, and I had the satisfaction of forwarding to the garrison as magnificent a piece of venison as ever graced a mahogany table. But to return to our friends, who are doubtlessly impatiently waiting to commence work. The dogs were thrown off, and but little time was lost before we had evidence that the quail had arrived. Die was the first to stand, and no sooner had she assumed her rigid position than both Doe and Sancho backed. Soon a bird was on the wing, and as rapidly cut down. More than an hour passed, with little other diversity than when bad shooting was made, and the luckless traveller would run the gauntlet of our crowd; many a good-natured joke and happy salvo of wit greeted the "wiping of each other's eyes," and our attendant coolies commenced to groan under replenished game-bags. What is there more delightful than a party of happy friends meeting to enjoy the paramount pleasure of a day's shooting? A person of great literary talent once wrote that the chase has a striking resemblance to war; for my part I cannot see it, for I never yet was under fire without feeling a nervous and a strong desire for the termination of the programme. I have heard many boast that they gloried in the whistle of the bullet or the wicked, venomous screech of the shell. Bah! I cannot believe such statements. Nature has not gifted me with less courage than my fellows; still, I never could overcome an unconquerable dislike to witness brains and blood scattered around, or a disfigured, inanimate form drop from the ranks, perhaps of one as unfitted as myself to go to his final reckoning. But what are the dogs about, standing as stiff as posts? and although we are close up, never a feather can we see. Heigh on! Good dogs! Not a step will they move! All our inducements can't make them advance. "Look out for a partridge!" exclaims our veteran leader; previous experience warned him what it was. One of our number headed the canines. Still nothing flushed; each tuft of grass is kicked; back and forth we walk, when, birr, with double the noise of an old cock-pheasant, and with a little of the rapid action of a high-pressure engine, Master Frankolin rushes, on rapid wings, for a new abode; bang! bang! speak the guns, and at last he is cut down; the less-experienced having missed their bird like men, and our veteran leader tumbling him all of a heap, the unfortunate victim turning a succession of somersaults ere the velocity with which he was going became fully retarded. I never yet knew a novice succeed in his first effort to kill this description of game, for their flight is so rapid, the rumpus they make on taking wing so great, and the whole performance so sudden, that the tyro is certain to get disconcerted. Have you ever witnessed the pace with which a flight of teal, with a gale of wind at their stern, descend upon a sheet of water? If so, their velocity is the best comparison I can offer. We had now evidently struck the haunts of the frankolins, for several more were killed, and not a few escaped scot-free. One remarkable peculiarity about them is, that you will never flush them in coveys; at the same time, where you find one, more may confidently be looked for. I remember once having crossed over to Kowloon, which is on the opposite side of the harbour, and on the mainland, to try and pick up a few snipe, as a *bonne bouche* to finish a repast I was about to give some friends. A good supply of No. 9 and my sixteen-bore I considered the most suitable for my purpose. Sancho, whom I had taught to retrieve, among other accomplishments, as the wet paddy fields are often far from agreeable to tramp over, was my companion. In crossing a ridge of rough ground that divided one flat marsh from another, he pointed respectively three frankolin, and although I was within easy shooting distance of each, and most thoroughly dusted their jackets, making the feathers fly, I had not the fortune to secure one. The vitality of this bird is truly amazing, and unless you break a wing, or otherwise render him *hors de combat*, you are extremely unlikely to see him again, for once he is started, he knows no bounds to his journey.

Onward our party continued. After picking up plenty more quail, our canines stopped on the edge of a slope densely covered with dwarf brushwood, principally composed of the beautifully brilliant azalia which grows here in the greatest profusion wherever the soil is moist. I cannot say I was surprised, for an internal whispering had told me what to expect. A brace of pheasants took wing, several misses were made, but the duo were knocked down; one quivered on the grassy open, while the other fell in the underbrush. The services of Doe were brought into requisition, and after losing a quarter of an hour, we were compelled to retire with only one bird. However, Doe was not satisfied, and he remained behind to make a final effort for the recovery of the wounded game, while we continued our work; in little more than ten minutes the sagacious dog joined us, triumphantly bearing the wounded bird, and so little was he injured by the setter's teeth that he made several abortive efforts to escape before he was safely deposited in the game-bag. That night, on counting our spoil, we found three pheasants, nine partridges, and almost a hundred quails—pretty good shooting, I think, you will agree, for four guns during an afternoon.

CHAPTER XXII.

DRIFTING TO DEATH.

IT is well known that a swimmer may incur considerable danger by bathing in the presence of a faithful dog, because the instinct of these animals causes them to believe their master is in peril, and by misdirected efforts, instead of saving, they complete the catastrophe they wish to avert. Such a misadventure once occurred to me, and as the circumstances were peculiar, the narration of the same may not be without interest.

While in China, on returning from drill in the afternoon, my house-boy informed me that a coolie had just arrived from Shangmoon side, and that both snipe and quail had arrived in considerable numbers. Such a chance for a day's sport was not to be disregarded; so hurrying over to the colonel's, I got the requisite permission to absent myself for a day.

At the Club House I mustered a couple of companions, neither of whom I had ever been with before, but as they bore the reputation of being good sportsmen and crack shots, I was only too glad to accept their society. Soon all preliminary arrangements were made; I was to dine with them, take a sofa afterwards so as to be up by break of day, and the earlier ready for a start.

With my dogs, for I had a brace, I turned up for dinner. The meal passed pleasantly, and a couple of arrivals (warm-hearted, chatty fellows), when the wine was placed on the table, dropped in and caused us to disregard the fleeting hours, till it was so late that we unanimously agreed not to go to roost but make a night of it—not a very judicious course for those who wished to make clean shooting.

With daybreak we sallied down to Peddar's wharf; the wind at the time was gusty, and the appearance of the fleeting clouds which scudded overhead ominous of a coming blow.

Now Pirates' Bay, where we intended landing, was a good six miles off across the channel which severed the island of Hong Kong from the mainland, a portion of which is a deep indentation in the land, enclosed on two sides by precipitous lofty hills.

But few boats were knocking about, owing to the earliness of the hour, and all which we hailed civilly declined to undertake our hire; at length, after considerable delay, a more adventurous craft came past, and after a little pressing and abundant promises of cumshaw, she was backed alongside, and we seated ourselves in the stern sheets, which were covered over with matting, to protect passengers from the sun's rays.

Before going further, it may be well to state that there

are no better boatmen in the world than the Chinese; the aquatic residents on that coast are at it from their infancy, and when they cannot go under canvas, Europeans had better take warning and douse their sails also. Well, we got on for a mile or two safely enough; a few small seas came over us, but more capable from their magnitude of damping our guns than our ardour; so forward for our destination we pushed, close-hauled occasionally, when the squalls freshened too much, luffing up a little closer to the wind.

Our boat was a stiff, weatherly craft, and with her reduced sail, and the comparatively smooth water that surrounded us, we had nothing to fear; but some persons will be fastidious—dirty particular, as a friend of mine used to say; so what should one of my friends do but insist on steering, because a few sprays had damped his well-trimmed and much-loved whiskers. Now these appendages were his treasures, his first thought in the morning, his last at night, and possibly received many a furtive glance during the day, whenever he chanced to be in the vicinity of a glass. It was of no use attempting to dissuade him from his resolution; all the arguments I could use to the contrary were thrown away; further opposition on my part I felt would lead to a rupture, so sooner than such should take place, I tacitly gave my consent for him to take the tiller-lines, the coxswain's seat, and become our Palinurus.

This change of steersmen was soon effected, and from the time it took place the gusts of wind appeared to freshen. For fifteen or twenty minutes we did well enough, at length a harder squall than had previously been experienced threw us almost on our beam-ends. "Luff!" was the word, and luff it was, till so much luffing was done that on righting to an even keel, the boat gibed, and being trimmed so as to sail on the tack we had pursued, the craft turned her keel to the heavens, and we went out from under the awning in what the fishes must have considered a most ungraceful and highly-ludicrous manner.

On coming to the surface and wiping the brine out of my eyes I was grabbed by the shoulder by our would-be helmsman, the one who had placed us in our present predicament, and, worse than all, he could not swim, nor would he leave go his hold. Argument and remonstrance were useless, shake him off I could not, selfish enough I should have been to try it; but a drowning man will grasp at a straw, and certainly from my personal experience he will cling to any one that can swim, whether he causes his destruction or not; so ceasing to exhaust myself by remonstrance, I struck out and gained the gunwale of the topsy-turvy boat, my friend clinging to me as tightly as ever did the old man of the sea to Sindbad.

At the time this catastrophe happened, the tide was running out, and there we were, for all managed to reach the boat, hanging on to our reversed cockle-shell, with my dogs swimming round about, every now and then paying me a visit, with the intention, evidently marked in their countenances, of asking how I was, and whether I required their assistance. But here our trouble did not cease, too many of us clung to the same side of the boat, placing more weight on it than on the other, and when an unusually high sea would sweep past, the boat would turn over and right herself, but from her great sheer it was impossible to bail her out, for the sea made a clean breach midships.

Again and again from this rotary movement we were all thrown from her, and as time elapsed, and all, dogs included, became exhausted, the latter would persistently come to me and endeavour to rest their exhausted bodies by placing their limbs upon my shoulders.

One moment the boat had her keel down, next upwards. When the former was the case, I used my endeavours to shove the unfortunate canines on board; when the latter position was in the ascendant, they had to swim, for the craft was deep and sharp, with but little flooring, and consequently little resting room to be obtained in the vicinity of her keel.

During every minute for a quarter of an hour our boat changed its position, and would doubtlessly have continued to do so but that we managed more equally to distribute the weight along each gunwale; but before that was accomplished, what between my friend clinging by me, and the dogs swimming to me, I was about "played out." At last the distribution of weight gave me release, the pets were placed inside, and my friend was given a good hold by the stern. Time fled on rapid wing, minutes became hours, already we had drifted by the familiar objects that mark the outer harbour of Hong Kong; Stone Cutter's Island disappeared from view, and still no friendly sail was at hand.

Although sharks are not particularly numerous here, I expected a bite every moment, because I had white trousers on. Not I alone, but all appeared to labour under the same conviction, nor did we hesitate to convey our conviction to one another. Our position was truly unenviable, for we were drifting out to sea before a rapid tide, and the only prospect before us, unless a ship should heave in sight, of outliving one another, depended on the amount of vitality each possessed.

Landmarks which I well knew glided past; farther and farther our temporary support drifted on; still no craft came to our aid, and truly we felt that we were alone on the bosom of the waters. At length one of our party, not he who had steered, spoke in serious words; they were to the effect that his strength was giving way, and he felt that in a few minutes he must relax his hold. I begged of him not to do so; I entreated him to show his pluck, reminded him of his wife and children, and how they depended on him for their support. My entreaties had their effect, for still he clung to the wreck. We must have been in this predicament over two hours, when a Chinese junk hove in sight. Closer and closer it approached, at length scarcely a hundred yards divided us, when up went her helm and off she stood upon another tack, alike disregarding our shouts and signals. My last hopes vanished with her. I felt convinced that I was now performing my last exploit. And when the heartless Celestials, whom I was sure had seen us, turned their rudder towards myself and companions, I hurled a deep and heartfelt anathema after them.

Our last hopes appeared to fade out with the junk; farther and farther she receded from us; at length her hull disappeared, and nought but the mat sails could be seen to mark her existence. Again and again I tried to reanimate my companions, no easy task, for both appeared to have lost hope, and with it the desire of continuing existence. My last effort had been made; supplications and entreaties were exhausted; I believed momentarily that one or both would have relaxed their hold, to enter eternity, for the ordeal was a severe trial of endurance, and one was far from being strong, the other without any knowledge of the art of swimming. As sea after sea broke over us—and with the passage of time they were becoming larger as we drifted farther from land—my dogs required more constant attention; scarcely would they be placed in the boat, resting on the seats, when a more angry wave than its predecessor would carry them beyond us; and they, poor creatures! would invariably swim back to me for help. Again and again this had been repeated, and I had almost ceased to feel capable of placing them in the submerged boat, when, as we drifted by a point of land, the extreme end of a diminutive island, a square-rigged ship, studding sails set, with her stem pointed at us, hove in sight.

With eyes strained almost to bursting, all gazed upon her; with over-taxed hopes, all prayed that she might not go by us: on—on—she came, stately with her majestic spars. But, alas! she veered to the right, and if she continued her present course, she would probably pass more than a mile from us. If the decks were deserted, if the watch were not on the alert, it was quite possible we might drift past unobserved. At length we were abreast of this vessel—no indication on her decks told us that her occupants were aware of our vicinity—what was to be done to attract attention? Each in his turn raised himself and shouted; but the weak and worn-out voices never reached their destination. At length one of the Chinese boatmen divested himself of his outer garment; he waved it in the wind, and just as our hopes of succour were dying out, a boat was lowered from the vessel's waist, several seamen sprang into her, and ere half an hour passed, we were all, dogs included, on board the 'Flying Mist,' on her passage from San Francisco to Hong Kong. At the gangway the captain met us; he was just such a man as it was desirable to come in contact with under such circumstances—hospitality occupied a large part of his big heart.

CHAPTER XXIII.

WILD DUCK SHOOTING.

A MONTH or more after the shooting incidents last narrated, after the manner of ardent devotees of the chase, when the ladies had left the table, and we had concentrated the sundry decanters at one end of the board, and lit, from the ever-ignited, smouldering joss-stick, our inimitable cigars of the brand of Contrabandistas, the most fragrant of all Manillas, conversation turned upon our mutual hobby. Long shots and short ones, heavy bags, strange adventures and shooting companions, were all discussed; even the relative merits of respective gunmakers fell in for their share of criticism, and so the happy hours fled with rapid stride, and even after the obsequious, trim-clad Chinese lad had several times announced that the ladies expected us for tea in the drawing-room, our topic had not become worn out; although courtesy demanded our compliance. However, I fear that we were far from gallant companions, for soon after imbibing the cup that cheers but not inebriates, we made our exit for the well-sheltered verandah, to loll with luxury in that perfection of lazy persons' lounges, loblolly chairs, with which every gentleman's household in that warm climate is numerously supplied. With the increase of cooling draughts, warmer got our theme, till at length we had definitely arranged that next day, weather propitious, we would start for Deep Bay, distant about thirty miles, to wage war upon the numerous ducks and geese which generally frequented that neighbourhood at this season of the year.

Now, this trip was a hazardous undertaking, and recruits had to be beaten up, for in numbers there is strength, and a jaunt in any direction exceeding a few miles was always extremely dangerous, and even more so than usual at this period, for a premium of three hundred dollars was on each European's head that could be sent to the Chinese government. Still, what will a sportsman not risk rather than be debarred the enjoyment of his favourite pleasure! Early rising, uncomfortable quarters, exposure to wet and storm, are all smiled at, and even the luxurious couch, the handsomely furnished chamber and *recherché* table, are often, for a period, temporarily foregone.

As my good old friend and companion had a deserved reputation for his success and knowledge of the haunts and habits of game, he had no trouble in procuring recruits; so that on the morrow, when, at the appointed starting time, I arrived at our place of rendezvous, two old friends were already on the ground, amid a pile of wine-cases, boxes of potted meats and vegetables, gun-cases, and all the etceteras of a sportsman's paraphernalia, discussing the prospects, and anticipating with pleasure the deeds of prowess we were about to perform. Soon we were all—four in number—transferred on board the clipper-built 'Lorcha,' and as her crew shook out her immense matting sail, the wind laid her over, the smooth water splitting before her sharp bow, and bearing us forward for our proposed destination, as soon as headway was obtained, at fully eight or nine knots per hour. Lounging on the deck in every attitude of repose, enjoying the balmy breeze and beautiful scenery that surrounded us, we quickly gain the Capsheemoon Pass, where the panorama, beautiful before, even improves; for countless are the rugged mountain-peaks and numerous the islands that form the background of the landscape, while innumerable craft of every size, shape, and nationality, glide swiftly by in close proximity, good evidence of the immense carrying trade of the interesting and strange inhabitants of this far-distant and little-known land. An old and favourite shooting resort, Castle Peak, bears on the right; while Linting, once the rendezvous of fleets of wealthy East Indiamen, looms ruggedly on the left, now long deserted and divested of the busy bustle of commerce for the safer anchorage and pleasanter island of Hong Kong. On, on we glide, with little change, save additional motion, for we are gradually gaining open, unsheltered water, till the skilful pilot deems we have made sufficient offing, alters our course, and bears up for Deep Bay, which, by the way, is very shallow as far as depth of water is concerned, and must have gained its name from the great distance it runs inland. With a good breeze upon our beam, we lay over to port, and rapidly draw in upon the shore, our sail level as a flat board, till scattered villages and numerous paddy-fields show, bespeaking the abundance of population and untiring energy of the industrious natives. Chinese villages are generally very picturesque, the style of architecture quaint and pretty, while the situations are always admirably chosen to please the eye, having abundance of scattered shade-trees and wood around. Which of us does not well remember the old willow-pattern on China ware, once so popular and universal? What child has not gazed with wonder and astonishment upon its bad perspective and curious details? Nevertheless, making allowance for all its faults, it has a marvellous resemblance to many a celestial homestead I have visited in my lengthened sojourn in that densely populated country.

Having advanced as far as navigation would permit at the then state of the tide, we grounded on an oyster bank, where we were compulsorily detained for several hours; and as the day was now too far advanced to commence work, cigars and other etceteras, with the additional accompaniments of pleasant companionship, did not cause us to regret the detention, and swiftly passed the hours, time being enlivened with many a merry song or sparkling joke, racy anecdote, or reminiscence of far-distant homes.

On rising before the sun on the morrow, we found our crew had not been idle, for we had advanced ten or twelve miles farther, and were now safely moored in the channel of a considerable river which flowed through the centre of a large rushy marsh, intersected in every direction by watercourses; in truth, just such surroundings as a duck-shooter would choose, and as we supped our morning cup of coffee in the twilight, flight after flight of the web-footed gentry whistled by, intent with preoccupied thoughts, and consequently fearless of danger, to gain some oozy mud-bank or sheltered feeding-ground.

After a consultation, it was decided that we should separate, two of our party going up stream, the remainder down; and as I and my worthy friend, the projector of this escapade, were assigned to each other's companionship, we soon crossed the bulwarks and seated ourselves in our skiff, behind four stout Chinamen, whose sinewy arms made the well-seasoned ash oars bend under their muscular exertions, while our stem was pointed for the more open water.

It would scarcely be fair to neglect to mention a very important personage who accompanied us, viz. a French poodle, who, in our estimation, and in the estimation of all who knew her, was supposed to know more than all the dogs of her day. This animal was an untiring swimmer, up to every trick, and comprehended almost every word that was said to her; still she was ladylike in being fond of having her own way, and even occasionally would display a most provoking amount of obstinacy. But being well acquainted with her peculiarities, I was induced to take her, as we were without a retriever, for I was aware that, if the spirit moved her propitiously, she would make herself most useful. As we proceeded rapidly down the stream, with a favourable tide, sundry shots were obtained and several single birds were picked up, but none of the flocks we had earlier observed had, so far, come within reach. My companion, besides his ordinary twelve-bore gun, had a double barrel of six gauge, from the well-known establishment of Egg, and as he had frequently used it with good results at long ranges, we both had great hopes of successfully bringing it into play. On approaching the more open water, a dense phalanx of teal were seen hovering over a mud-bar, and with powerful stroke and keen expectation we directed our course for this miniature regiment. Again and again the ever-varying flock rose and descended with rapid swoop, the light glancing off their metallic-coloured plumage as if from a mirror, and recalling remembrances of the appearance of a flight of golden plover. As teal in these waters are seldom wary, no care was taken to conceal ourselves. The only caution we adopted was that the Chinamen lay on their oars when we had obtained good headway, which, with the force of the current, rapidly hurried us forward. Yard by yard we steadily advanced till but sixty intervened, and the ducks, which had previously alighted, indicated symptoms that our presence was disagreeable. D. pitched his gun, and two reports followed with little interval, the first shower of shot being delivered while the birds rested, the second as they hurriedly rose to quit so dangerous a neighbourhood. The result was that thirty-two plump beauties were bagged, with at least a fourth more disabled, which were unfortunately lost; a termination which too frequently follows long shots from large guns. The bar which we had now reached appeared a favourite resting-place for wild fowl, and in little over an hour more than a dozen of the web-footed genus were added to our already extensive bag. However, as day advanced, the game became more wary, and we consequently determined to go on a voyage of discovery in quest of fresh scenes and less-watchful ducks.

The tide was now out, and as we glided along the shore of numerous slobby mud-banks, we observed sundry Chinamen gathering shell-fish over the treacherous, oozy surface. Their manner of progression was novel and curious. Each searcher had an apparatus like a large hand-sleigh, with an upright at the back extremity, on which he leaned his chest, propelling the vehicle with his feet in rear. Nor was this all. Ducks and geese, which were feeding in thousands on these slippery banks, did not appear in the least to regard the presence of John Chinaman, while plying his avocation; long association, previous security and uninterruption, had gained these wary birds' confidence, and with simply a flutter or quack, they cleared the path for the shell-fish hunter to progress. No man with the smallest amount of invention could fail to turn such a discovery as this to advantage. D. had been a sailor, and well knew all the intricacies of knots and splices; a couple of these hand-sleighs lashed together, with a seat between them, was all that was requisite, but to make the trial less liable to failure it was better still for the gunner to don the outer raiment of a native. Having consulted one of our oarsmen, who spoke our lingo, we made arrangements for opening negotiations for the temporary use of these novel machines, and quickly had a couple alongside our boat. With many an intricate and skilfully devised knot, brace and counter-brace, the construction was fabricated; my friend had already put one of the boatmen's common garments over his own—no easy matter, for he was portly, in truth very portly, though short in stature—and with his redoubtable heavy gun, he determined on making the first essay. Before starting, however, an additional improvement was suggested, viz.: a stool for him to sit on, which was received with approval, renewed ties and bights being placed around its legs to keep it firm in the proper place. Never shall I forget, to the last day I live, the imposing appearance of my companion, as he started with a smile of satisfaction on his lip, and an injunction to me not to let the cat out of the bag when we got home, as the escapade could be repeated on the morrow. With two of the lusty Chinamen propelling him forward over the slimy surface, with rapid, sleigh-like motion, ere going much over a hundred yards, a shot was obtained, and six or more curlew were cut down at short range, ignorant from where came the death-dealing hand. Soon all were gathered up, and "*en avant*" was the cry; but whether it happened from the knots being insecure, or the lashing breaking, or the propelling force not acting simultaneously, dreadful to narrate, the two mud-boats parted, and my stout, jolly, kind, good-hearted friend disappeared between them into a bed of the foulest, softest, most beastly filth that ever edged a sea-girt shore. If my fears were great, the consternation of both the attendant Chinamen was even greater, and if they had dared, doubtlessly would with the first impulse have deserted their frail and treacherous crafts rather than bear the brunt of the irritated barbarian's wrath; but go they could not without their boats; their locomotion was stopped, and with assumed submissive aspect, they resigned themselves to the force of circumstances. D. plunged and snorted; never did war-horse, in all the glory of his strength, or mired buffalo, with all his power, perform more astonishing feats of prowess and agility. First one leg and then the other was withdrawn, each in its turn to sink deeper as weight was placed upon it to assist in regaining the lost throne of eminence. Danger being out of the question, I could only lie down and laugh at the absurdity of the whole affair; nor for the life of me could I do aught else. Never, in the course of my life, could I remember seeing so close an approach to the perfection of low comedy. Protracted and violent was the struggle, and when at length dear old D. had regained his seat, the comicality was none the less, for from head to foot, over face and hands, was the black, slippery, ill-smelling matter, completely obscuring features, and hiding entirely the colour of his garments. The cherished fancy of his brain, the possession of innumerable wild fowl, had fled, and all the treasures of a hunter's cupidity were now but vanity, the essence of vanity.

What a spectacle did he present, mud from head to foot! Even his gun, the powder-flask and shot-belt which were suspended around him, had so changed their shape and appearance that the most astute never could have recognised them! There are some persons so physically constructed that it is impossible for them to suppress laughter when aught risible strikes their fancy, and so it is with your humble servant. I should have been extremely sorry to forfeit the friendship of my friend, and I was aware that to be made a butt of was his horror, and would probably cause him much annoyance. Still to witness his rotund figure, besmeared countenance, and woeful expression, as he was propelled towards the boat was so ludicrous, so absurd, that I was obliged to give way to my feelings. Old Neptune, grown as hoary with sea-grass as a ship's bottom after a five years' cruise, could not have figured in a more comical light.

Of course our shooting for that forenoon was at an end, and in no loquacious humour we retraced our way to the 'Lorcha.' Poor D. being outraged at my want of sympathy, disgusted at my heartlessness, and in a bad temper with his own lack of skill and discretion, brooded over his misfortunes, and nursed his wrath till he should come across some one on whom to vent it. As we approached the craft, our friends were seen on deck, who naturally anxious to learn of our success, rose to receive us, but no sooner had their eyes rested on the mud-stained sportsman than peal after peal of laughter resounded, each more violent than its predecessor, till both appeared on the verge of a fit, and as their hilarity increased so did D.'s wrath, till, unable to suppress it any longer, he poured a volley of abuse on his China boy, who was assisting to unrobe him. However, D.'s rage was like a summer's shower, of short continuance, for after he had undergone a good tubbing and change of raiment, and imbibed a drink and lit a cigar, his jolly old phiz was illuminated with a smile, and as he narrated all the particulars of the escapade, he laughed as heartily as his listeners at the absurdity of the whole affair.

That afternoon I started alone to look for snipe on

the paddy-fields, and was most successful, for the game was abundant and tame, the weather being mild, bright, and warm. These enclosures are eminently suited for snipe-shooting, as the ground is clear and unobstructed, for each is small and divided from the other by a flat bank, on which the walking is good. As I advanced, bird after bird flushed, of both the painted and common species, till my game-bag was expanded to its most capacious limits. As the evening drew on, several bunches of teal passed within gun-shot, of which I was able to make a good score, till I was ultimately obliged to cease by the weight of my burthen. The sun was now setting, and admonished me that it was time to return, and as I turned my steps homewards, the view which presented itself, illuminated by all the rich glow of a tropical sunset, called me to a halt. The better to appreciate its beauty, I rested upon a rock, and still think I never enjoyed a more lovely panorama. Verdant, well-cultivated land, with numerous hamlets of snow-white cottages nestling under the giant foliage-covered branches of many varieties of trees; a still, placid bay, unrippled by the most gentle breeze, formed the fore and middle-ground; while distant irregular mountain-peaks, marked by deep contrast of light and shadow, composed the distance—the whole forming a picture worthy the skill of any artist—but still there was a want, a necessity, not easy to be supplied—no lowing herds of cattle, no happy groups of children, no industrious farmer unhitching his companion horses, or frugal housewife, or healthy dairy-maid relieving the patient cows of their milky stores, such as is seen at home, broke the monotony. With all the gorgeousness of tropical flora, all the brilliancy of tropical light, still on every Eastern scene there is a stamp of semi-barbarism, semi-civilisation that cannot fail, in the eyes of all, when we think of our native land, to detract materially from the foreign picture, unless the spectator be one of those unhappy beings whose existence has been a blank or series of misfortunes, inducing him to abhor all that may remind him of the ties that bind the heart to home, nationality, and friends.

That evening, one of our crew, who had been on shore, brought us the startling intimation that a piratical junk was in the neighbourhood, that they were aware of our presence, and intended, during the night, paying us a visit. Of course, such a warning was not to be disregarded, and steps were forthwith taken to afford us the best chances of making a successful defence. The neighbourhood bore a bad character, and the conduct of the few natives with whom we had come in contact plainly showed that their feelings towards us were far from amicable. Moreover, but a short time previously, a yacht belonging to a wealthy mercantile house, on a trip from Macao, with none but her Chinese crew on board, had been captured, all the hands killed except one, the craft run ashore, pillaged and stripped of her copper; and, although every exertion had been made by the gunboats, the marauders were still at large, and were believed to reside in this neighbourhood. After seeing that the watches were properly set, and cautioning our crew against surprise—for on them we had the greatest reliance, the inhabitants of Hong Kong and those of the coast, although of the same nationality, being always at bitter enmity with each other—we retired to our crib to reload and overhaul our arms, that they might be in the most effective state if called upon for service. With danger many become reckless, and the prospect of using our guns on larger game than wild fowl did not prevent us from passing a jolly evening. The jovial cup went round and round, and cigar after cigar was demolished, till the atmosphere of the close cabin was so dense that the figures of companions loomed big and indistinct, the smoke appearing as if it might have been cut with a knife. All went merry as a wedding-bell, and half-an-hour more would have placed us in the arms of Morpheus, when the shrill clear voice of the watch on deck was heard challenging some unknown intruder. With one impulse we all tumbled up the companion, to learn the cause of alarm, which soon was obvious, for about a hundred yards astern loomed the figure of a large junk. Now, whether this was only a trader or a robber was doubtful, but time would show. During this delay, D., who from age and experience was acknowledged commander, instructed me to look well to the masthead, and if I could see a figure there—a position always secured on such occasions by a villain with a stink-pot; a piece of crockery containing liquid fire which ignites when thrown upon the deck—to pepper him with both barrels of his heavy six-bore gun, loaded with swan-drops.

Slowly and steadily the supposed foe advanced, till within thirty paces, when she bouted ship at being challenged, and lit a port fire. The light soon illuminated both their deck and ours, giving a good view of the numerical strength of both parties; but whether the supposed foes were disappointed with our appearance,

or were not what we suspected, they gradually paid off to the wind and rapidly disappeared from view. From our ignorance of the language and manners of the Celestials, it would be difficult to come to a conclusion whether their intentions were hostile or not, but our crew continued to insist that they were undoubted lallaloons.*
The excitement of this little incident had banished sleep, so instead of retiring, we determined to make a night of it, the better to be prepared for another visit, or to be earlier ready for the morning shooting. Before day broke, wild fowl were distinctly heard upon the wing, and as a considerable change had taken place in the atmosphere, indicated both by our own feelings and an observable fall in the thermometer, sharp work was expected. The duo who had gone up the water being well pleased with their previous day's work, preferred their former beat; so D. and self started downwards, for the bank near which we had killed the teal. On our way we cut some rushes to form screens at the most favourable stands. All this time, although day had scarcely yet broken, flock after flock hurried past, but from the uncertainty of the light and the probable difficulty in gathering the slain, we desisted from shooting. On rounding the last point of land that severed us from our ground, our patience was doubly rewarded, for thousands of birds sat upon the water and beach, pluming and dressing their feathers in conscious security. Nor did they appear to regard our presence, for many, and those closest to us, remained with their heads under their wings, dreaming doubtlessly of far-distant northern haunts upon the banks of the Amoor, or others of the

* Pirates.

numerous rivers that pursue their solitary course through the sparsely populated plains of Siberia towards the Arctic seas. Getting good way on our boat, the oars were unshipped, and a preconcerted signal agreed upon for opening fire. Foot by foot we steadily approached, till but thirty-five paces intervened, when each aiming low, our two right-hand barrels responded to the pressure on the trigger, cutting a lane through the unconscious broad bills, and as they rose, almost with the voice of thunder, off the water, each left-hand barrel repeated the performance, bringing down in all attitudes maimed and wounded. Over thirty birds fell to this fusilade, and among their numbers was to be found almost every variety, from the handsome plumaged widgeon and teal to the larger mallard.

Except on American prairies, in autumn and spring, at the periods of migration, I know of no place where such fine duck-shooting can be obtained as here; but the preference, even if the numbers should be much less, must be given to America, for few of our race can continue to breathe the noxious miasmas that night and morning arise from the paddy-fields without his constitution and health becoming seriously impaired. In fact, two of the gentlemen who then shot with me found premature graves, and in each instance their medical attendants affirmed that they had contracted the disease which had deprived them of life by their too-frequent trips in pursuit of their favourite sport.

Our work commenced successfully, and how often does a good *début* tend to make us continue to perform well; both shot better than usual, and it soon appeared that we had but to point our guns to cut down the swift-winged game. Later in the day, finding that the boat alarmed the birds, we placed our screens, and dismissed it to wait till wanted. The poodle that I have mentioned did excellent work, entering quite into the spirit of the sport, and appeared perfectly delighted at the fun of retrieving and wooling the dead, dying, and cripples. As time advanced, the birds became more wary, and frequently would alight just beyond gunshot. However, I adopted a plan which succeeded admirably, *id est*, toling the game up.* The poodle's greatest pleasure appeared to be in carrying stones which had been spit on, more particularly if large and almost impossible to get in her mouth. Now this little eccentricity I turned to advantage, for I kept her busy on the beach, lugging, hauling, and fetching. The movements of the dog evidently excited the curiosity of the duck, for when they would perceive her, they would bunch together, and swim towards her, curious to see what all the fuss was about, nor would they halt till within easy range. Again and again was this device practised, till nearly two-score birds had been killed. But the dog's retrieving qualities were soon tested too severely. A cormorant, which is about the size of a goose, and provided with a most formidable hooked bill, with which it can bite most severely, came skimming by ; with the same feelings which cause the sportsman always to shoot at a hawk I gave him a barrel, and tumbled him over with a broken wing. The poodle was sent to fetch him, and after a long chase succeeded in collaring the bird. But the cormorant didn't see it in the same light, and bravely

* A common method in America, and frequently very successful.

resisted; both wings and bill were brought into play, feathers and wool flew; the dog was determined, and so was the bird. A more perfect example of "pull devil pull baker" scarcely could be imagined; first one had the advantage, then the other, till Master Canine succeeded in getting the bird by the neck and triumphantly landed him. But one pill was a dose; the poodle had never previously been so roughly handled, and all my future efforts ever after failed in making her carry aught that bore feathers.

On joining my companion, I found he had done almost as well as myself, for conjointly we could number over seventy birds; and as the sun was getting too powerful to be pleasant, we started for our 'Lorcha,' which we soon gained, having the assistance of a favourable tide and wind. On getting on board, we met our friends, who had also done well, and, as our stock of game was as great as we could make use of, without a single demur we hoisted anchor and set sail for Hong Kong, which, without accident, we safely reached that evening, in time to enjoy another social evening and fight our battle over again.

Persons residing in or visiting Hong Kong can always in winter enjoy a good day's duck-shooting if they take a trip through the Broadway, or Southern passage, which leads up to Canton. So great is the quantity of birds to be found there that I have been informed on no less authority than that of a naval officer once serving on that station, that he killed over a hundred birds at one discharge of a small carronade loaded with duck-shot.

CHAPTER XXIV.

FIRST HURDLE RACE IN JAPAN.

"LET go the anchor," when sung out by a cheery voice, is most melodious; and seldom are the words unwelcome. On the occasion to which I allude they were not, and as the chain rattled out through the hawsehole, as if in echoing response to the Commander's voice, making the ship reverberate from stem to stern, I believe there was not one soul on board that did not feel thankful, and why? Twenty-four hours previously we had been tossing about off Cape Itsu, in fact between it and a dangerous archipelago of islands, of whose peculiarities we had no chart, while the wind was raising as big a rumpus as it is possible for it to get up; indeed, blowing a regular typhoon, accompanied by such torrents of rain as are only known to the visitors of the tropics. During the day we had passed up from the outer to the inner bay of Yeddo. Previous to this trip, I had sworn by the beauty of the Dardanelles, vowed by the grandeur of the Bosphorus; but all my previous expectations, aye, though impressed upon me by such language as issues from the unmatchable Byron—fell to the ground when I beheld the constantly changing panorama of the termination to our voyage. Can I describe it? —I will try. The foreground of the picture was composed of the most placid cerulean-blue water, the intermediate of the most variegated and beautiful woodlands, intersected by numerous openings, all rejoicing in an apparently abundant harvest, while superbly magnificent and ever-beauteous Mount Fusiama backed the distance, distinct, but soft in outline, regular in shape, as if the production of some giant mathematician; while the summit sides were intersected with frosted rays of silver (the snows remaining from the previous winter), that looked like the airiest and brightest plumes that ever graced the hat of fair lady or gallant general. You may be a wanderer from youth to the age allotted man to live; yes, you may travel the world from pole to pole, visit every nook, every corner of this earth, and I doubt much whether a more beauteous, more grandly magnificent scene can be beheld from shipboard than such as is seen as you pass the narrows that lead into the inner bay of Yeddo!

Scarcely had the reverberated echoes of the descending anchor died away when a host of European visitors arrived on board; the majority sought news. A small clique sought me, and what for?—to get me to act as clerk of the course, at a proposed race-meeting, the first ever held in Japan, and also to ride a horse. To the first duty I readily consented, to the second it is possible I should have objected, but when the petitioner was a big-hearted American, who had, under the instructions of the gallant Commodore Tatnall, then commanding the American fleet in Chinese waters, assisted to tow many of my countrymen from under the destructive fire of the Tachoo forts, when through treachery our little fleet was so sadly discomfited, I struck my opposition, and promised to do the best in my power to bring his horse in a winner.

In Japan—it was so then, I believe it is so now, and trust it may ever be the case—the best, warmest of kindly feelings existed between the American residents and the representatives of my own land. The race-meeting had been determined on by both nationalities, and our kind, good-hearted consul at Kanagawa, once an officer in the Guards, had been selected for judge. The ground chosen was only a short way from Yokohama; the Japanese authorities had assisted in laying out the course, and, considering the time and opportunities, had succeeded in making a suitable place of operations in no ways discreditable to their ingenuity and the occasion.

The early races of the meeting passed off to the satisfaction of all, the Japanese officials kept the ground free from intrusion, and entered with the greatest pleasure into the sports. It might be three o'clock, perhaps later, when the saddling bell sounded for the grand performance, that in which I was to figure, nothing less than a hurdle race, with about eight flights in a mile. Up to this period I had not seen my mount, still I felt no uneasiness, for I was assured he was a good one, who only wanted some one on his back to make him go, and that with such he could jump anything, from a five-barred gate upwards.

The competitors, nine or ten in number, had assembled; their costumes were more varied than picturesque, but still my nag had not put in an appearance. Better late than never, at length he came, and, O shades of Rosinante, what a brute! not out of condition certainly, but such legs, and as long as if they had been supplied with stilts from *les Landes*. Moreover, he was as light in the body and girthing, yes, and more so than any weedy screw that ever looked through a halter at home, while his temper was such that the horse-coolies who led him were kept constantly on the *qui vive*.

To mount took me several minutes, and I doubt if I should have succeeded but for the application of a twitch. I tried a preliminary canter, but found it no go, and inwardly I wished my acquaintance—I won't say what or where. In the meantime I had taken measure of my antagonists; of one only had I anything to fear; his mount was far superior to my own; the remainder I expected would kiss mother earth at the first fence. My conjecture was correct, as the result proved.

The starter tried to marshal us in line. I had drawn second place from the inside, but to occupy it was the difficulty. I made one or two attempts, and in doing so endangered all I came near, so at last I retired to the rear; when doing so my steed seemed to think that he had gallantly acquitted himself, and as a reward should be allowed to go home. It was no use my differing in opinion, the Latchfords had not the desired effect; the more I plied them the harder he backed. He had got his legs in for the retrograde action and would not exercise them otherwise. At length I got two horse-coolies, each armed with a telling bamboo, to take Rosinante by the head, who were further instructed, when the flag fell, to lay on the beast's rump with all the *vim* that their biceps possessed. It was my only chance to get under way. The first hurdle was a rasper, stiff and strong as logs and wattles could make it; but by this time so thoroughly had my determination been aroused that I believe I would have rushed him at a *chevaux de frise*.

The flag fell, the ruck started, and, bang! bang! went the canes over my steed's extremities. Well under his flanks I got my spurs, and if nothing more suffered, the hide certainly did. The locality my nag thought considerably too warm, so with a buck jump and a couple of lashes at the coolies he followed his competitors.

How the first fence thinned out the aspirants for turf honours was beautiful to behold; only one got over safe, the one I had previously supposed the most dangerous. At the jump I rushed; the vixen rose at it, and then appeared to change his mind. The impetus, however, took the forequarters over while the hind ones remained on the obstacle. With hand, spur, and whip I got him over, very much, I think, to the brute's surprise, for as soon as all four legs were again on *terra firma*, he struck out into a good wholesome gallop, requiring all my power to keep him together. The sole survivor and only remaining antagonist was at least a hundred yards ahead. The ground was soft—very soft, I may say—and his nag was going with a slack rein, yawing about like a ship at sea, the rider anywhere to be found between his mount's ears and tail. The second, third, and fourth hurdles were jumped by both successfully. The gap I did not try to close—to do so would have smothered any chance I possessed; therefore I put my trust in Providence, and hoped for squalls. As my antagonist approached the second last hurdle, I saw him using the steel freely and his horse's tail go up.* He reached the jump, bungled, and nearly fell over it. My mount was still fresh, for I had kept him well together. This hurdle I got over swimmingly, which I hoped the foe would fail in doing when he came at the last. Providence had so ordained it, for if ever a man came a cropper and made a breach, such was done on this occasion, and I cantered through the gap up to the winning-post before my adversary had wiped the stars out of his eyes, for he had got such a purl as previous experience had told me generally illuminated our optics with an extensive view of the planetary system.

I was glad to win the race for two reasons—firstly, that I might hand over to the owner the purse; and, secondly, that my reputation as a steeplechase rider should not suffer in the eyes of a crowd of griffins.

* Generally an indication of exhaustion.

CHAPTER XXV.

VOYAGE THROUGH THE JAPANESE INLAND SEAS.

UNFORTUNATE indeed must be the man who has no memories to recall of unalloyed happiness! In the calendar of my life no part so thoroughly deserves to be marked with a red letter as the months I passed in the realms of the Tycoon.

There are few more beautiful views to be seen than surround the beholder who stands upon the deck of a vessel anchored off Kanagawa. To the right extends a straight line of coast in the direction of Yeddo, thickly wooded almost to the water's edge, and closely dotted with the clean, neat, and picturesque residences of the inhabitants; to the left the coast-line sweeps round with abrupt curve to Yokohama, green bluffs dotted with foliage, giving a charm to the scene which is heightened to perfection by the glorious towering summit of Mount Fusiama, grand in its size, magnificent in its altitude. Like a potentate, it appears to rule all the surrounding country.

From a distance Fusiama looks as if it were a solitary excrescence in the centre of a vast plain; but such is not the case, for numerous hills, which elsewhere would be worthy of attention, help to make portions of the base of this wonderfully shaped sacred mountain.

The first time I saw this mountain was under most advantageous and peculiar circumstances. Our vessel having been caught in a typhoon the day previously, as we were doubling Cape Itsu, the violence of the wind, the near approach of night, and our captain's ignorance of the rocks, currents, and islands, that abounded in the vicinity (for in those days no trustworthy charts of this coast were to be obtained), induced him to order the ship to be put about, so as to obtain an offing till favoured with daylight. And well it was that he did so, for the winds and waves held high revels, and the rain descended as if the flood-gates of heaven had been opened; sail after sail was taken in, neither watch obtained their allotted period below, and our noble vessel strained and groaned under the severe lashing which the disturbed elements vouchsafed her.

With little warning, except a sudden fall in the barometer, the storm commenced, and it terminated as abruptly, for when day broke the wind had died out, the waters had subsided, and the atmosphere was unusually clear. Not having undressed during the night, as our position was one of considerable danger, the first faint lines in the East that ushered in the rising of the sun found me on the poopdeck for the purpose of enjoying a cheroot and a cup of coffee.

As the sombre shades of night chased each other to

the westward, and the sun had nearly approached the Eastern horizon, before us, on our port-bow, appeared the summit of Mount Fusiama—the base being wreathed in clouds. Its colour was of the palest blue, except where snow rested in the ravines; its shape a triangle, with the upper point squarely cut off—a staff officer's cocked hat, with its numerous, white, streaming plumes floating from the crown, is the nearest simile I can think of, to convey to the reader a good idea of this distant charming vision.

After spending some weeks at Kanagawa, where pleasure had predominated over work, the *yamoon* of our Consul being my principal residence, I received orders to proceed to Nagasaki, on board one of the P. and O. steam-vessels chartered by Government. Instead of following the coast, the inland sea was to be our route, and three Japanese pilots were sent on board by the Custom House to superintend our navigation. One or two Dutch and English men-of-war had previously passed through this landlocked channel; but with these exceptions, we were about to visit localities unknown to Europeans. With break of day we got under steam, rejoicing at the prospect of adventure and novelty; on the bridge, calm and serious with the responsibility of their position, sat the three subjects of the Emperor; between them rested their compass and their charts.

The outer and inner bay of Yeddo is connected by a channel much resembling the Bosphorus, with the exception that the line of shore is not so precipitous and rugged, while the vegetation is of a deeper green and more abundant. The bluffs that margin the waters of the grand Mississippi before its junction with the turbid Missouri have often recalled to my mind this far Eastern locality. On gaining the entrance to the outer bay, our stem was pointed to Simoda, where we arrived in a few hours, and came to anchor. As our stay was uncertain, none were able to leave the ship; but abundant amusement was obtained by pistol practice at the numerous divers that constantly were floated past in the tideway.

Two sharks, about eight or nine feet long, honoured us with their presence, and appeared carefully to examine the ship, which, no doubt, they regarded as a new species of sea-monster with which they had no previous acquaintance; but their inspection was brought to an abrupt termination, for one of my companions gave the larger a pill from his Colt's revolver, which struck near the junction of the vertebræ with the head, thus at the same moment terminating its curiosity and its life.

From the appearance of these fish, I should pronounce them to be the common blue shark, sometimes seen in our home waters, and frequently to be met with all along the Atlantic seaboard of the American continent.

The following morning, with a fresh and fair breeze, we tripped our anchor and headed for Cape Itsu. The nearer we approached that inhospitable, bleak, iron-bound headland the fresher it blew, and when we had at length doubled it, on altering our course to the southeast, we found ourselves opposed to a heavy gale, and a most uncomfortable short tumbling head sea; moreover, the barometer continued to fall rapidly, an indication that an unpleasant night was before us. Hereupon the pilots, beckoning the captain to them with various pantomimic gestures, gave him to understand that shelter had better be sought. Our course was now changed several points more to the east, sufficient fore-and-aft canvas was set to steady the vessel, and in a couple of hours we were approaching what appeared the ugliest piece of coast-navigation I had ever set eyes on. The Japanese still coolly retained their positions on the bridge; not a word escaped them, and nought but an occasional wave of the hand to the men at the wheel indicated that they were possessed of life. On our part, all felt most uncomfortable; doubts and fears would constantly arise in our minds that these swarthy Orientals might be mistaken as to locality, or purposely running the ship on shore.

Half a mile did not intervene between us and a long, apparently unbroken line of sunken rocks, the loftier of which would occasionally show their heads through the hollow succeeding an unusually large wave. Closer and closer we approached, and just as we imagined destruction was imminent, a clear channel of blue water became apparent, through which we threaded our way, immediately afterwards entering between two bluff headlands, one of which was crowned with a detached rock, much resembling a martello tower, into a beautiful, calm, narrow bay, running quite a couple of miles inland.* At the upper end of this bay, shut in among green hills, and close to a most picturesque village, embedded in trees, and embellished by a handsome temple, we dropped anchor. It

---

* The entrance to this bay in more than one respect reminded me of the entrance to Balaklava Harbour.

would be difficult to say whether the surprise of the peaceful inhabitants at our appearance, or our own at the sequestered tranquillity of the pretty spot we had reached, was the greater. Evidently our advent was regarded with great suspicion, for no visitors came near us till evening.

In the meantime I went ashore with my gun, landing several hundred yards from the village. Along the margin, in the wash of the miniature waves, were feeding numerous flocks of waders, several of which I killed, but without finding a new species. I remained for some minutes on the margin of a stream, close to where it entered the sea, admiring and amused by a colony of land-crabs. Immediately on my approach, they would retreat to their holes, in a few moments returning to see if the intruder had departed. These small crustaceæ are evidently largely gifted with curiosity; they are of a most active and quarrelsome disposition, and possessed of insatiable appetites.

On ascending to the higher grounds, which were covered with beautiful dwarf azaleas in abundant blossom, I much regretted being without a dog, as I saw plenty of convincing proofs that pheasants were numerous, and probably then lying *perdus* in the timber that grew along the ravines and watercourses; however, a frankolin gave me an easy shot, but so unexpectedly and rapidly did it flush that I missed it with both barrels.

After a wearisome climb I reached the summit of the nearest hill. The view was grand in the extreme. Beneath my feet the angry sea, white with foam, lashed the iron-bound coast, while behind the undulating lands were cultivated with a care and neatness that at once predicted abundant crops as the probable result of good husbandry.

The few inhabitants that I met, who previously had possibly never seen an European, regarded me with awe and astonishment. One whom I tried to ask for a light refused to hold communication with me, but slowly retreated backwards, muttering something unintelligible between his teeth, and finally made rapidly off, stopping every moment to convince himself that either I was not following or that he was not dreaming.

On my return homewards, close to a spring, I killed a frankolin; the sandy edges around the water bore proofs that some of the deer family were in the habit of coming there to slake their thirst. Near the confines of cultivation, where the arable and wild land joined, a cock copper pheasant crossed me, and dropped into some millet. As I did not feel justified in trampling down the grain, I could not get him again on the wing, so unwillingly relinquished the search.

On arriving at the ship I found it surrounded with native boats of every shape and size, and filled with hosts of occupants of both sexes, all apparently decked in holiday garb. One of the pilots had been on shore; he had evidently reported favourably of us, and hence this influx of visitors.

After considerable palaver, some of the notables were induced to cross the gangway; their manners were dignified, yet gentle and unobtrusive, and their astonishment at the vessel's magnitude, at her engines, and, lastly, at our saloon and cabin, was more than funny—it was serious. Half an hour's sojourn convinced them that nothing was to be dreaded from us, so that the tabooing we had previously suffered from was removed, and all that were so disposed were permitted to come on board. They were an excellently behaved company, for though on every hand were ranged what to them were wonders, still all were satisfied with looking, and abstained from touching. Would my own countrymen, under such circumstances, have been equally considerate?

The gilt buttons of our military clothing particularly attracted the young ladies; women are as fond of finery in Japan as at home, and never was brilliant ring coveted more by city belle than were these ornaments of our costume. Having more than a dozen spare ones below, I distributed them to the best-looking. The treasures were accepted with a timid, bashful grace, while a brilliant blush suffused their faces. These fair ones, particularly when young, are very pretty, and not nearly so dark as the sterner sex. How they laughed and giggled as we showed them different articles of our apparel, and when a glove was placed on one of their hands, all fairly screamed with pleasure! The dress of the Japanese women, both north and south, is almost the same; the richness of embroidery, material, and ornaments denoting their rank. It is strange, but nevertheless true, that the costume of our "girl of the period" much reminds me of the millinery fashions prevailing in that distant archipelago.

Bottles, tins, in which meats and condiments had been preserved, were welcome gifts, a wine-glass or tumbler a most valuable present; and with such odds and ends all went away loaded, not forgetting to leave in return little souvenirs quite as valuable in our eyes. Unluckily the assassinations of Europeans that have occurred in this distant land have given stay-at-home persons the impression that the Japanese are treacherous and bloodthirsty; my experience has taught me to believe exactly the reverse, for, although they are proud, high-minded, and recklessly brave, they are kind, hospitable, and gentle. And I believe that, when they have used their weapons against their Western visitors, some imaginary insult, or some mistake resulting from ignorance of their habits, has been the cause of provocation. English and Americans, as a rule, are too prone to treat all with dark skins as inferiors, and therefore browbeat, bully, and even strike those whom Nature has thus painted. Such I know to be the case, and have on more than one occasion been surprised to see the admirable command of temper the injured persons have displayed.

Leaving our shelter at daybreak, by midday the estuary that commands the entrance into the midland seas was reached. Bungo Channel is, I believe, the name it bears. Many whales were seen during the run, and report says that it is a favourite breeding-place for these mammals.

As the land gradually closed in, cultivation and numerous villages became apparent, and as far as we could judge, prosperity and happy peaceful homes were scattered far and wide. How different is this from China! All the result of the labour of man's hand there is in a state of decay, speaking of past grandeur; here all is in perfect order, clearly telling of present greatness.

In Japan agricultural implements may be more rude and primitive than in Europe, their invention and manufacture less complicated and highly finished, still they are suited to the wants of the population, and as they know no better, they are satisfied. Having within their reach the summit of their ambition, we have a right to expect that they are happy. For my own part, I believe them to be as happy and contented a population as is anywhere to be found on the face of the earth.

Another characteristic which cannot fail to strike the stranger is their extreme cleanliness. All classes appear equally to love washing, and to practise it. Even the coolies and lowest grades invariably looked clean. Their last work, when the labour of the day terminates, is to wash off the perspiration and filth that results from their toil.

While on deck, watching with pleasure the ever-changing panorama, my attention was called by the boatswain to a scene I had frequently heard of, but never before witnessed. In fact, previous to this day, I had believed that such only existed in the productive imagination of lovers of the marvellous. It was a contest between a whale and some threshers. I do not say thresher-sharks, because I believe the fish I speak of and the well-known species which bears that name are different.

The sailor's yarn goes on to say that the sword-fish and thresher enter into an alliance, hunting in couples. When these allies fall in with the whale, he of the sharp nose pokes the unhappy monster up from below, while every time the unfortunate blubber-coated gentleman comes to the surface the thresher, springing from the water, falls upon his back. Thus between the two, the persecuted whale is forced to disgorge his food, on which the unprincipled colleagues feed.

The scene I beheld was certainly sufficiently similar to permit the fabrication of a more extraordinary story. But we were too far off to witness the details, which must have been well worthy of the observation of all enquirers into the minutiæ of the economy of animal life.

The entrance to the Inland Sea is apparently well fortified. The smoothness and landlocked appearance of the water within make it resemble one of our Scotch lakes. Several of the views, looking through vistas of well-wooded islands, were really beautiful, and the lofty mountains in every direction, softened by climate and distance, made a charming background.

At sunset we anchored in front of a large town, densely populated, with numerous handsome yamoons surrounded by trees close to the shore. Half the population appeared out for a holiday, for the water was covered with boats, all the occupants being in gala dress. Few minutes elapsed after the anchor was down before we were surrounded by the astonished crowd, who advanced closer and closer, till unfortunately the engineer permitted the escape of the waste steam, which so intimidated all, that the most ludicrous scene of confusion occurred in their efforts to gain the shore.

The next day, under weigh by an early hour, we recommenced threading new intricacies and beholding fresh beauties. Towns and hamlets were scattered on every side, while large junks floated by or lay at anchor. I think we are still very ignorant of the resources and population of Japan, and that it is possible, by a closer contact with them, for us to learn, from this great Eastern people, much which might be of benefit to our over-populated island. The town we next anchored at to spend the night must have been inhabited by a branch lodge of the far-famed Rollicking Rams. Off they came in scores to greet us, chanting their impressive songs to the time of the scullers who propelled their boats.* Many of them had grog with them, which was willingly tendered for our consumption; still, although *saki* is not a bad tipple, our Japanese friends showed a marked preference for what we had. They kept going and returning till so late an hour, that prudence forbade any more visitors being received. Long after midnight I heard a party on shore singing, not "We won't go home till morning," but, as my imagination told me, a correspondingly festive ditty, suited to the longitude of Japan.

During the remainder of our journey, the same scenes of loveliness, the same hospitable receptions by the people, were repeated, so that we were all fascinated with Japan and her inhabitants. And when anchor was dropped in Nagasaki Bay, I can safely venture to assert there was not one on board who did not wish to have the same cruise over again.

Before leaving this highly favoured and charming country, I will mention that many of our evenings were spent in witnessing our horse-coolies wrestle. They had built a ring, a little larger and much resembling a cockpit, which they floored with sand, and in this they performed their deeds of prowess.

* Boats are always sculled in Japan, not rowed.

Having several Devonshire and Cornwall men with me, I induced those that professed a knowledge of this art to enter the lists. They did so, and invariably were thrown; and it was done with such apparent ease, and always by antagonists less than themselves, that I actually imagined that our countrymen did not exert themselves. At length I could stand it no longer. Determined to do credit to my race, I entered the arena as a combatant. For a long time no foe offered. Afterwards I found my rank was the objection. However, after much palaver, a little fellow—very little indeed—was coaxed in. Numerous were his salaams, expressive of the honour I, a Yaconin, was about to do him in accepting him for an antagonist.

Wishing with all my heart that this mosquito of a fellow had been twice the size, we embraced. With but little exertion, I threw him. Again we laid hold of each other for a second trial. The tables, however, were turned, and I found myself sprawling on mother earth without knowing how I got there. A third time the second performance was repeated; and I retired crestfallen, while my successful adversary carefully brushed off from my clothes every speck of dust, and mumbled unintelligible words expressive of the honour he had received.

I feel now convinced that this little creature permitted me to throw him on the first occasion, hoping that I would then be satisfied, and not urge any more trials.

Possessed of the greatest admiration for Japan and the Japanese, I predict they will yet rank among the most enlightened nations of the earth.

CHAPTER XXVI.

EL DORADO.

CALIFORNIA, of which San Francisco is the mercantile capital, is so much changed of late that the reader must not go there now with the expectation of beholding the scenes that frequently occurred a few years back.

The discovery of gold in any part of the world has always had the effect of drawing together crowds of the dissolute, idle, and " ne'er-do-wells." Ballarat, in Australia, passed through a similar ordeal to San Francisco, in California. Nor can this be wondered at when it is known that the gold fever invariably first seizes the bad and reckless of every nationality.

Because California is a portion of America, I would not for a moment have the reader to imagine that the education and proclivities of the people of the United States have anything to do with the reckless and anti-law abiding scenes that have taken place on the Pacific slope.

Commerce was prosperous, gold plentiful, new "leads"

daily reported, and the influx of immigrants into this El Dorado was immense at the date of my visit. Money was so abundant that it was no unusual thing to see a pinch of gold dust tendered for admission at a theatre door. The fever for excitement ran high, and gambling became an overruling passion with a large portion of the community. Having no intention of remaining in San Francisco, I only made such a stay as would enable me to procure necessaries that were absolutely required for carrying out my future projects.

Against gambling I would warn all. I have been guilty of the vice, and have repented my folly. Do, therefore, as I recommend, not as I have done.

One evening, when the performance was over at the theatre, wishing for further excitement, as the night was yet early, I consented to go with a friend to a gambling-house which received a large amount of patronage from the heterogeneous population. Faro was the game; and after witnessing the proceedings for some minutes, I made a bet and won. Again and again the operation was repeated with like success. Luck evidently appeared on my side; and ere I arose from the table, I was the winner of a considerable sum. I retired with my gains, and next evening returned to the same work. I was not successful on this occasion; and as one or two disputes had taken place, I resigned my seat, but remained as a spectator. In the same room where Faro was being played, a select few were indulging in a favourite American game called "poker." The players were of strongly contrasted appearance. One was handsome, and sufficiently aristocratic-looking to represent the oldest Anglo-Saxon family; another, olive-brown in complexion, might have sprung from the Hidalgos of old Spain; a third had "villain" stamped upon his countenance, while the rest were more commonplace, or possessed less distinguishing characteristics. A remark made by one of the party induced me to overlook their play. A short stay informed me that the ill-favoured person was winning. His manner at once told me that he was in better society than he was usually accustomed to. Again and again his gains were drawn in by him, and some vulgar joke or a proposal to stand drinks followed each of these proceedings. To a casual observer, all apparently were satisfied; still I observed a sterner expression settling on the face of the handsome contestant. Once or twice he made remarks on the provoking pertinacity of adverse luck; yet I must say that he lost his money, apparently, without regret, and with the most gentlemanly *sang froid*.

My interest had become excited, and consequently I felt inclined to see the affair out, when to my astonishment I saw the person whose appearance had elicited my interest, with a rapidity that was surprising, drive through and pin to the table with a large clasp-knife the hand of the common-looking fellow who had been previously winning. At the same instant a revolver was pointed at the head of the cheat (for such he was proved to be), and a wholesome piece of advice given him that, if he attempted to stir or draw a weapon, his brains would spatter the wall.

In a moment all was uproar and confusion, all the occupants of the room rushing towards the point where, like statues, stood the principals. On the face of one was stamped cool determination to do all he said, on the features of the other flitted vindictive malice, accompanied by spasms of pain, arising from the wound he had received.

The owner of the establishment, who in turn officiated as barman, banker, or croupier, was a powerful, burly, bullet-headed fellow. He is still, I believe, alive. With the voice of a bull, ferocity and decision being equally apparent in it, he laconically asked, "What's the cause of this muss?" "Search this blackguard's sleeve—that of the hand I hold pinned to the table; the villain has been cheating all night, till I obtained this opportunity of exposing him!" quietly but firmly uttered the fair-haired stranger. True enough, two cards were found; indignation became rampant, and some benevolent parties considerately proposed to lynch the delinquent. However, the cur escaped, and doubtless, if alive, vividly remembers the lesson he then received.

Game in California was then very abundant; and as I always possessed a strong preference for out-door life, especially when shooting could be enjoyed, day after day I wandered off at an early hour, often not returning till after dark. A voyage along the coast, when the weather permits, will produce abundant amusement; for seals and sea-fowl are to be found everywhere, and fish are extremely numerous. But leaving the water, inland was generally my selection; and what a shooting-range was there! Every sheltered valley swarmed with birds—the California solitary partridge, mallard, duck, teal, and snipe, being the most numerous; while deer were far from uncommon, and hares dodged in and out of every patch of brush. Scarcely a day passed without somebody seeing a grizzly bear, and seldom a week elapsed without accidents from their pursuit being reported. Near Sacramento I met a cavalcade. The specimens of humanity that composed it were of the very roughest description; regular "leather-stockings," in all the glory and attractiveness of greasy, dirty, well-worn buckskin clothing. Between them they led, or rather dragged along, an unfortunate mammoth grisly bear, cut, bruised, and apparently half-starved. The hardy rough mustangs that each of the wild mountaineers bestrode exhibited plainly that theirs was no easy indolent life, that short commons and hard work made up the greater portion of their existence. Yet their eyes were bright, and they raised and replaced their feet with an air that clearly indicated good health and powers of great endurance.

Although fossil remains of horses have been found in America, there is nothing to justify the supposition that these quadrupeds existed on the Western Continent when first visited by Europeans.

Soon after, however, Spanish horses were introduced, and all those to be found in Texas, Sonora, and California, ranging about wild, have the form, shape, and peculiarities of their European progenitors.

But to return to the capturers of bruin. I passed the night with them, and a daring, reckless crew they were. All, with the exception of a Milesian, were descended from families that had settled in Missouri when that State was a territory and formed the western boundary to civilisation on the American continent. Each was over six feet high, straight as a lath, spare, muscular, but powerful, ready either to fight Indian or Catamount at the shortest notice.

One of this party had his face bound up, and an arm in a sling. This—and his being by some years the older—enlisted my sympathies, so I volunteered to stand him a drink. Even bad whisky will unloose the tongue, and, when not too frequently taken, promote feelings of good fellowship. Hitching up his belt, and producing a plug of tobacco, nibbled around like a ship-biscuit that had been left in the way of rats, he took an enormous chaw, offered me the balance to help myself from, and then spoke thus :—" That's an almighty big bar ; he's not perhaps the heaviest I have seed, but by long odds he's the tallest ; and when his dander is riz, you had better believe he's all there ; and we had the hardest kind of time in fixing him. It was him that chawed me up, smashed my arm, and near took my scalp off, till this hoss most thought he was a dead coon. A Greeser (Mexican) that lives on Bolt's ranche knowed this bar for many a day, for he would just come round the homestead and help his-self. Bars have a wonderful amount of sense ; they know a Greeser, they does. If Missouri or Kentucky folks had been living on that ranche, he wouldn't have come it that style, you bet. Well, I and the boys come across his track, but for two days we seen nothing of him. At length, when out berrying, I ran most agin him, for the critter was on the same errand. We both seen the other together, and he riz on his hunkers, grunted, and jist as I thought he was on to me, he gave a snort, and made tracks as if skeered. You see, stranger, that bar seed I was no Greeser. Well, I didn't shoot, for an old load was in the rifle; and altho' she do carry plumb centre, she jist wants to be kindly treated to be relied on; so I went home and wiped her out, after which I came back with the boys to the huckle-berry patch, but the bar had gone; and we giv up looking after a bit, thinking luck was agin us. Scattering over the place to get a feed, for the berries was prime, as I stepped out from behind a log, jist facing me, looking as pleased as a well-fed nigger at meeting an acquaintance, was the grizzly. Quick as a steel trap I drew a bead, fair plumb on his breast, atween the shoulders; darn me if I didn't think to drop him in his tracks, but I didn't hold straight. A kind o' buck fever must have been over me, and before I could turn he was on me like a wild cat. The first sweep he gave raised my hair; the next I knowed, I was doubled up under him, and the plaguy critter was chawing my arm. I tried my best to get at my bowie, but I was that cramped I couldn't reach it. But the boys heard the shot. Up they come, Jake first—that big un standing with his back agin the fire there—he's a bully boy, he is; and he let drive. However, the shot didn't drop the varmint, but it most did as good, for it took the plaguy critter off me, and after them; but they give him it hot and strong till he caved in; and as they thought he might be playing possum, they muzzled him, and tied his legs; and so it proved, for you see he's not a darnt bit the worse, altho' he's got five shot-holes in him. Why the boys didn't kill him, you see, they thought that a heap of dollars might be got if we took him all right into Sacramento or San Francisco."

Q

The party were not wrong in their conclusion, as I afterwards learned. The last I heard of poor bruin was that he and a bull were pitted against each other to form the object of attraction for a choice assembly of brutes met together on a Sunday afternoon.

After a delay of some months in the hills, a report of gold being unusually abundant in Sonora caused me to direct my steps southward.

CHAPTER XXVII.

A DAY IN SONORA.

SONORA! What a euphonious word. I never listen to it without pleasure, for it recalls both music and the dark-eyed beauties of Andalusia; but Sonora is far from old Spain, across the Atlantic, across the North American Continent, bordering on the placid margin of the blue Pacific.

The catalpas, a tree far excelling in fragrance and beauty the horse-chesnut, were in blossom as I threaded my way along a path just discernible from the surrounding savannah. My horse was foot-sore, leg-weary, and heartsick, for he had performed a long and tedious journey on soft food, while my saddle had badly galled his withers. Poor faithful steed! It bled my heart to mount you in your distressed condition, but I had no alternative. Day after day, as lassitude became more apparent in your limbs, and your once bright eye became more filmy, I frequently argued with myself the charity of turning you loose to wander at pleasure;

but if I had done so, you never would have reached a settlement, possibly you would have been devoured by wild animals, and I should not have been here penning your troubles and my respect for your memory.

The country through which for some days I had been travelling was open park land, bounded on the east by rugged hills. Game was abundant. Hares (*Lepus townsendii*) quitted their form on every side, coveys of Californian quail *(Perdrix californii)* flushed almost under my horse's hoofs, while the fleet antelope *(Antilocapra)* bounded past, swift as the wind. But a listless stupor was over me. I cared not for the most tempting shot; my gun was a nuisance to carry, and but that it might be required for protection, I believe willingly it would have been dropped.

And why, you will ask, had I got so reduced in pluck? Simply for this reason: I was suffering from an attack of fever and ague, a disease difficult to get rid of, and one which of all others depresses the spirits most, and makes the victim reckless and careless of consequences; moreover, the despondency of the horse, perhaps, was imparted to the rider, for it was really a doubtful matter which of the two felt the most sorrowful and woebegone.

Thus the day had glided by; all nature was bright and cheerful; every animal, tree, and shrub happy and fresh-looking under the invigorating influence of the early summer sun, making the contrast between the travel-stained wanderer and sweat-soiled steed the more conspicuous and disparaging. At length the increasing shadows told that it was time to choose a halting-place—a matter of no great difficulty, for the surface of the country was so similar that, excepting you chanced to seat yourself in a nest of ground cactus, there really was no choice of situations. Attending first to the wants of my horse, and relieving his poor back as much as possible by changing the position of the saddle, I turned him loose to obtain his supper. Having disposed of this duty, the all-important fire was my next thought. There was plenty of wood around; still I could not find any sufficiently dry and inflammable to start a blaze, and so in pursuit of this necessary material I wandered almost a mile from my selected camping-ground. As I advanced, on opening from the sparse timber to the grass land, a hundred yards to my right, I observed over a dozen wild cattle assembled in a close body, with a splendid bull, the evident leader of the troop, stationed about forty yards in their front, facing towards the timber, lashing himself into a fury with his tail, tearing the sod with both hoof and horn, and expressing unmistakably that mischief was brewing. In juxtaposition, still and braced, stood a grizzly bear, angular and starved in looks, with a coat so ragged and unkempt that at once I concluded he was either a time-worn veteran or the victim of some slowly consuming wound.

Both foes were so intent on the other that I had little difficulty in obtaining a favourable position for viewing the action that was pending, for bruin evidently meant mischief, and the bull appeared no way loth to accept the gauntlet.

A short time before, over the camp fire, I had listened with great interest to a genuine mountain man—one who had passed a lifetime on the eastern and western slopes of the Rocky Mountains—as he described such a rencontre as was about to take place. Little then did I suppose I should have the fortune to witness one of those scenes seldom viewed but by the venturous naturalist, hardy trapper, or skulking aborigines.

At length both foes appeared to consider that time was up. The bear, with quiet measured step, had lessened the intermediate space, and fire flashed from the bull's eyes. With a sudden spring and head lowered, the latter rushed to the contest, and was received by bruin in a half-erect position, the fore-paws being used as buffers to lessen the concussion. However, the force nearly bore him to the ground, but his tactics now were changed; his immense claws were fastened in the bull's withers, and all his strength was exerted to prevent the head of his antagonist being raised. Long and doubtful was the struggle. The success of the bear appeared to depend on his being able to retain his grip, that of the bull in getting free, so that he might procure impetus to renew the charge. Thus far I doubt if bruin had been punctured, whereas the blood flowed profusely from the hold he had established on his antagonist. When the contest had been continued some moments, the bull dropped on his knees; down, down almost into the earth went his head; but this was but a ruse to obtain purchase, for with the celerity of a steel spring upwards went his head, and the bear was thrown clear several feet. Master Grizzly would now have declined the contest if optional; but no such idea was in the mind of the foe, for after backing a few strides, with lowered head and irresistible force, a second charge was made, fairly driving the discomfited and disappointed marauder to a headlong retreat. The rest of the herd, who had stood aloof earnest spectators, now joined in the pursuit, and—would you believe it?—I, sick, weary, and footsore, found myself following up at the tail of the hunt at the best pace I could command, and I doubt not occasionally yelling a view halloa. For a mount that would have enabled me to see the termination I would have given a good deal; as it was, my locomotion was so slow that both pursuers and pursued soon were lost to view.

On returning to camp, to my surprise, I saw a stranger closely examining my trifling traps that had been left on the ground. Unperceived, with great interest I watched his proceedings. Having apparently satisfied his curiosity, he lit his pipe, and made himself comfortable, when a few moments after I walked up to him. On inspection, he turned out to have the most cut-throat expression I ever previously beheld; so much so that I at once concluded that he was one of those villains outlawed from the settlements, living as best he could, and even taking life if anything could be gained by it—for such characters were far from uncommon then in this locality. Our greeting was laconic and to the point, and in the very plainest possible words I told him that his society was disagreeable; however, he was not the person to take a hint or feel insulted: provokingly he listened to all I had to say, but showed no disposition to change his quarters.

At length the night wore on. I ate my meal in silent dignity, while my visitor kept talking incessantly, although I never vouchsafed an answer. About the hour when I would have gone to sleep he was joined by a comrade, a half-breed, if possible, more repulsive-looking than himself They evidently were associates of long standing, and sundry were the meaning glances I observed pass between them. Not relishing my situation, I determined to be particularly guarded and on the alert.

Once or twice the half-breed arose, and, making some paltry excuse, endeavoured to establish a position in my rear, which I frustrated; ultimately I informed both that any renewal of such conduct would at once provoke hostilities. With obsequious politeness they assured me my alarm was needless, that it was insulting them to express suspicions, that they were persons of undoubted respectability and character; but there was an unnaturalness in their assertions, a suspicious restlessness in their manner, a watchfulness upon all my movements, of which none but a fool could fail to see the import. Thus midnight was reached. More closely I drew my serrape about me, the watch-fire was reduced to embers, but all my tendency to sleep had vanished. With one hand I had inserted the bowl of my pipe into my bullet-pouch, for it performed the duty of tobacco-bag also, when several voices, at a considerable distance, jabbering Spanish, were heard. Sharp as my ears were, still more 'cute were those of my would-be companions; with a spring both were on their feet, and next second in full retreat. The spirit of the devil almost tempted me to take a flying shot at them as the last glimpse of the scoundrels disappeared in the darkness. There was something so comical in the precipitancy of their flight that I could not help laughing, at the same time congratulating myself that I had easily got rid of what I was certain were dangerous parasites. In a few minutes

I was joined by the Sonorians; without difficulty I learned that they were in pursuit of two men who had committed robbery and all but murder. With a collection of all the words of dead or modern languages I could command, I assured them that they were certain of success if pursuit were promptly carried on; that at best the villains had only a few minutes' law, but, with the apathy of their race, all came to a halt, dismounted, and huddling over the fire, smoked in silence; and if I reverted to the subject of pursuit, a yawn, stretch of the arms, and "*mucho fatigato*" was my answer.

In the morning, before leaving, I picked up a piece of paper from the place where renegade No. 1 had been seated, the edges of which were scorched as if the remainder had been used to light a pipe; this scrap was a portion of a letter. The few words that were indited on it spoke a volume:—" Shall I still continue to address your letters to Sacramento? remember what anxiety your absence causes me. My son, do return, for you are all an aged mother has to live for.—MARTHA."

Away beyond the limits of civilisation, where no laws exist, how many reckless, desperate, hardened villains are to be found; yet many of these men have mothers, sisters, and wives pining away life in the hope of a return which is destined never to be realised, for the career of the object of their solicitude has been such that the summary treatment of lynch-law would be instantly awarded them if recognised in any frontier settlement or seaport, thereby cutting them off from the rest of the world, and a chance of leaving those associates who first led them to wage war on their fellow-men.

CHAPTER XXVIII.

THE PARKS OF AMERICA.

IT is not to artificial grounds made, decorated, and enclosed by man's labour, that I wish to draw attention, but to enclosures far more secluded, far more extensive, and infinitely grander—the emanation alone of the great Creator.

In America are to be found many tracts of land in the vicinity of the large cities that can compare with the parks of Europe, and in one or two instances most favourably, but it is away from the busy haunts of man, away from the hum and bustle of commerce, out of sound of the murmur of population, across the Mississippi, across many hundred miles of prairie, to the sequestered, luxuriant meadows that lie between the eastern and western ridges of the Rocky Mountains that I would carry the reader.

The Rocky Mountains, which form, as it were, a backbone to the great North American continent, are divided into numerous ridges, between which are situated the parks I wish to describe. A river generally runs through each of these, the banks of which are fringed with verdant meadows, of less or greater width, girded around with gentle slopes, which increase in steepness and barrenness as they grow higher and higher. In these park lands a delightful evenness of temperature is generally enjoyed, for the surrounding elevations shut out the cold blasts of winter and the heated breezes of summer. Moreover, snow never lies on them long, and the melting of the glaciers in the summit ridges produces an abundant supply of water throughout the dry season. Nearly every description of vegetation which grows in the Western States is to be found on these enclosed plains, and from the atmosphere being moist and humid it flourishes with great luxuriance.

Some of the parks are situated on debatable ground, between two hostile Indian tribes, and they frequently then become the scenes of fearful conflicts. Again some reckless braves in pursuit of game will wander from their tribe, and take up a residence in a park the property of another race. A general mustering of the rightful owners will consequently take place to repel the intruders, for the Indian is jealous of his landed rights, and more especially of those territories which constitute their best hunting-grounds.

Numerous white men, sometimes alone, more frequently in small parties of two or three (more especially in old times, when a beaver-pelt was worth four times its present value), have spent years of their lives immured in these seldom-visited wilds, the events and experiences of one day being so similar to its predecessor that the passage of time would be unnoticed, till the size of their packs or the reduction of their supplies of ammunition told them that the trading fort must be visited. Instances have not been wanting of men turning perfect hermits, and isolating themselves from the outer world in some of these spots, trapping game for food, and using the bow and arrow as their weapon of defence. I once met a Frenchman who had devoted himself to such a life. His residence was on a diminutive island, in the centre of a small lake, formed by an obstructing beaver-dam, which caused an overflow. With a primitive log canoe he passed to and from the mainland. By chance I came across him setting a snare for some of the numerous *Lepus* family. He had not noticed my approach, and he started when I spoke, turned round towards me, and drew himself to his full height, wheeled to the right-about, with the precision and bearing of a soldier, and would have gone, only I detained him by laying my hand on his sleeve. With a gesture of impatience, defiance flashing from his eyes, he a second time faced me ; in his countenance was a look (it might have been the result of madness) which plainly said, "Trifle not with me." After a moment's pause, he muttered in clear, sonorous, haughty accents, " Pardon, Monsieur," and soon afterwards the last of his tattered clothing disappeared behind some intervening brush. How I longed to question him, to ask him of his previous history, the cause of his solitude! That he was a soldier, I had no doubt—one of rank, I thought probable. The military air, intonation, and look were all his ; why, I cannot say, but I feel convinced that he was one of those extraordinary men who sprang up and passed away with the First Napoleon, to whom a word of praise from their Emperor was the greatest honour. From a trapper who frequently visited this locality, I learned that there had been two of these isolated unknowns, but that one had long since disappeared. Doubtless the tax gatherer, Death, had taken possession of the tenement of the missing refugee. Possibly, after all, he might have been no hero, but an outlawed villain.

If man occasionally wanders to these parks to pass the sunset of life, the wild animals of the forest and plain do so likewise. The giant buffalo bull, grand in his proportions and magnitude, fierce in his aspect, from his matted, dishevelled, hoary coat, when no longer able to retain place with the migrating herd, and contend successfully for the choicest herbage, or the favours of the dusky fair ones of his race, seeks out these retreats, to pass the remaining portion of his days amid plenty, free from the dangers, bustle, and excitement which he so thoroughly enjoyed before decay had placed its stamp upon him. Poor old fellow! he now looks gaunt and ragged, but well he may do so, for only conceive the life of incident and danger he has passed through! From the day when his mother anxiously guarded him, with all the maternal solicitude that generally characterises the brute creation, when the grey wolf and cayotte prowled in their rear, willing but fearful to make an onslaught on the parent and child, to the period when he reached maturity, and possibly fled with countless thousands of his fellows, before the sons of man, ever too prone to shed blood ; or when later in life, fierce and ardent, he fought and subdued those less powerful than himself, and triumphantly carried off, from numerous claimants, the lady of his choice, from day to day, from year to year, constant and unremitting adventure has been his lot. But the sun of his existence is now declining towards the horizon; but a short period is before him ere his whitened bones will alone remain to tell the passer-by that once he existed. Look well, traveller; perhaps, even now, those clumps of buffalo grass conceal some foe, desirous enough to make a meal on the veteran's carcass, but fearful to risk a contest in which the issue might still be doubtful. I have never gazed on the teeming herds of wild buffalo which I have frequently encountered on the plains of the far West without thinking how wonderfully they differed in habits, bearing, and inclinations from domestic cattle. On the latter is planted indelibly the brand of serfdom; on the former, of reckless independence. In fact, each look what they are—the one the servants and property of man; the other free agents, conscious of their power, conquerable by death alone, the untrammelled and unsubdued children of the boundless demesnes of the Creator.

Whether it be that age causes animals to become reckless, or that their lengthened sojourn in the world has familiarised them with their strength, and imparted to them a knowledge of their powers of destruction, or that the lassitude resulting from infirmities causes their tempers to become soured, I know not. But when the old bull buffalo has separated himself from the herd, and retired, as it were, into private life, he becomes most pugnacious, and fearlessly attacks all intruders; fortunately his activity has deserted him at this soured portion of his existence, and but little exertion is necessary to avoid

THE PATRIARCH'S ATTENDANTS.

his onslaught. I once saw one of these hero-veterans die a natural death, an unusual occurrence, for their enemies are numerous and always ready to attack them when in that weak state that precedes dissolution. Well, my hero was standing on a mound, a setting fiery sun slowly dipped the western bounds of the landscape behind him, and made his huge outline loom doubly grand. Food had been scarce with me, and consequently I made a more than usually careful stalk to get within range; the game's position was such that I almost doubted the possibility of success, yet closer and closer, without causing any visible alarm, I advanced. At length, when I had decided that the range did not require lessening, I felt convinced that I had been seen; for the head and eyes were turned towards me, but no angry shake of the horns, paw of the ground, or flash of the eye evinced hostility, and, moreover, the figure appeared to lessen with each respiration, and an air of incapacity for further exertion was indelibly stamped upon the veteran monarch of the prairie. My gun was for the moment forgotten, and I gazed with wonder, and possibly with sorrow, at the apparent approach of death. By degrees the veteran's fore legs were placed farther and farther apart; rapidly diminishing strength instinctively compelled this method of supporting the towering figure; at length the body swayed, and, with a lurch like a foundering ship, rolled on its side, and life departed from the carcass at the same moment. Up to the termination of the career of the noble brute he had remained upon his limbs, defying decay with his last breath. With sorrow I looked upon the body, regretted that life had fled; although, at the same time, I had been drawn to the spot with the intention of executing the office in which I had been forestalled. Befitting was such a death to the greatest hero, succumbing only when nature refused to grant further support, yielding up the life and strength he had gloried in without a sigh of regret.

Sometimes the cow buffalo also finds her way to these parks; when she is about to become a mother, she finds herself, through weakness, unequal to the exertions necessary to keep up with the ever-travelling herd; but when the ordeal of child-birth is over, and the offspring is able to contend successfully for the necessaries of life among its fellows, both mother and baby wander back to the great plains, to attach themselves to the first herd that chance throws in their way.

Such a cow and calf, when met, are a prize of great value to the hunter; both are generally in the best condition, and fit food for the daintiest epicure; but the mother is strong and fleet, so is the child, and if the sportsman's horse have suffered from short-commons, or a dose of overwork, the owner may as well relinquish, without trial, all hope of ranging alongside of them within shooting distance.

Deer also visit these abodes of shelter, as well as the buffalo. The wapiti, handsome in shape, noble in size and bearing, and strongly resembling our red deer of the Scottish Highlands, abound in these mountain-fastnesses. From the luxuriant grasses and shrubs that grow in the low grounds they obtain abundant food, on the sloping irregular declivities, they have playgrounds that delight them, and on the upper crags that form the boundaries, safety from pursuit is within easy access. So seldom in these solitudes do they hear the report of a gun, still less see man, that not unfrequently they will advance towards the hunter, every lineament of their features marked with curiosity, surprise, and even indignation; but this is only when the cause of their inquisitiveness is to leeward of their position, for should the relative situations become changed, so that one breath of air tainted with man's presence reach their sensitive organ of scent, with the speed of a race-horse the neighbourhood will be deserted, for the protecting monitor, Nature, true to her darlings, whispers warning words, so impressive that they are never for a moment disregarded.

The life of deer, when free and untrammelled by walls and boundaries, must be more than usually happy; without care, and perfectly independent, their wants are easily satisfied; their food is the fresh crisp vegetation, and their dwelling-place the boundless plains or the picturesque mountain sides; while the air they breathe is unpolluted by noxious gases tainted with man's inventions and manufacturing instincts. They bathe in the brooks at will, sport in its pellucid current, love and are loved; and being without ambition, they commit no offences, which afterwards fill a guilty conscience with painful remorse.

After a stormy night, during which I had not obtained an hour's rest, first from the determined efforts my horse continued making to break away, and, secondly, from the torrents of rain that descended, my bivouac-ground being very exposed, I took my double-barrel Dougall rifle,* and, while my nag was enjoying his morning meal,

* A low trajectory of 14 bore.

I determined to see what addition I could make to our larder. The uneasiness of my animal was soon explained; bear-tracks were found abundant in the vicinity, and the imprints were so large that any brute of peaceful habits must of necessity have a dislike to the possibility of making an acquaintance with such a bruin. I closely surveyed the neighbourhood in the hope of introducing the contents of my low trajectory to Mr. *Ursus ferox*, but I was not in luck. The atmosphere was delightful, every respiration appearing to imbue me with fresh powers of walking, so I wandered on, for I had no fixed course, and entered a piece of open timber land. The birds carolled forth their morning prayer, the industrious agile squirrels skipped from limb to limb, occasionally halting to chaff me for my travel-stained and begrimed appearance. Even the snakes were out in force, but one soon gets used to them, and dreads them so little that a kick from your long-booted foot is frequently the only notice they receive. In fact, all animal life was having a jubilee; and the foliage, bright with autumn tints, and the grasses, brilliant from the late rains, formed a suitable playground for their frolics. Lost in thought and admiration, I was recalled from my dreams by a stone, at a distance of over one hundred yards, rolling down a declivity, and crushing the brush in its course. Anxiously looking round for the cause, before me I saw standing a splendid wapiti, nearly five feet high at the shoulder, bearing a head of horns not under forty pounds weight, and considerably palmated. The stag saw me, yet appeared unalarmed, for he arched his back and stretched himself. Advancing closer towards him, not so much with the object of lessening the distance of range as to see how near I could approach without alarming the animal, to my surprise he struck the ground with his fore foot and showed every indication of a disposition to dispute my rights of intruding into his demesne. But, poor creature, he knew not the fearful odds he had to contend with. Sixty yards now only intervened between us, so I pitched my well-tried friend to my shoulder, and ere the smoke had cleared off the ground, his beautiful dusky form was lying prostrate, apparently dead. Having reloaded, a performance that should be always enacted immediately, and before moving one inch towards your game, I advanced with my butcher-knife drawn to cut his throat. Depositing my rifle on a bunch of grass, straddling the victim, I raised his head, the keen edge soon brought blood, but ere the incision was an inch deep, the wapiti rose with a bound to his feet, giving me a tremendous purl; the deer at the same time almost pitching on my prostrate body, his shoulder being tremendously smashed. On the spur of the moment I made a grasp at one of the hind legs, which I succeeded in seizing, and, having severed the hamstrings, I prevented his escape and his power of doing mischief. Leaving my filthy rag that did the duty of pocket-handkerchief fastened to one of the horns, to warn off wolves, for these skulkers are ever suspicious, I returned to camp for my horse to bring home the game. It was almost sunset before I was back where this little adventure took place. The spot I had marked well in my memory, and my bump of locality I believe is unusually large. Already I saw a tree that I recognised; my quarry was only a few yards beyond it—yes, there it was, but in possession of one whom I had no doubt would refuse to listen to priority of ownership.

Over the carcass lay an immense grisly bear, his lips curled up so as to show his teeth, while a couple of grey wolves with watering mouths looked on, at a respectful distance. Dismounting, I fastened my horse with the lariat line, and unperceived, for I was favoured by the wind, I stole within forty or fifty paces of the would-be thieves. Bruin had evidently just arrived, for the carcass was intact. The presence of the wolves evidently was disagreeable to him, for although for a moment he would lick the blood-stained parts around the throat, every now and then he would lift his head, fix his diminutive eyes upon his attendants, and raise his upper lip so as to expose a powerful set of grinders. For ten minutes I watched this picture; at length the bear rose, and, laying hold of the dead deer by the nape of the neck, showed an evident intention of carrying off the plunder. As day was declining, I determined without further delay to assert my claim. A good broadside shot offered itself, and with the report my foe fell to rise no more, and the brace of skulkers made tracks for safer quarters.

In these retreats an animal is said to exist which the mountain men very much fear, and call a carcaju. Frequently at night I have heard the most unearthly howling, such as, when once heard, can never be forgotten, and I have been informed that it emanated from this creature. From description I believe it must be nearly allied to the caracal; but why should it be dreaded, unless much larger and more powerful than that animal? One of my temporary companions, a half-breed Frenchman, who was considered an excellent hunter, returned to camp one day earlier than usual. From his manner I saw that something unlooked-for had occurred; and when questioned, he informed me he had seen a carcaju. On enquiring why he had not shot it, he appeared to think that any attempt to do so would be futile, and probably lead to his own destruction.

A few days after this I made an early start to visit a stream where beaver signs were extremely numerous. On my route across a rocky spur, I saw a couple of bighorns. These must not be confused with the Rocky Mountain sheep, for the animals that bear these names among the western hunters are perfectly different, although both belong to the goat family. They, however, frequent the same localities, the *habitat* of the latter possibly extending farther north. Both these races are the most wary, and consequently the most difficult game to stalk on the American continent. Descending at break of day to the lower grounds to feed, ere the sun has dried up the morning dews, they are *en route* for the highest and most inaccessible crags. Sometimes, as you thread your way through the rocky canons,* away, hundreds of feet aloft, on a pinnacle of crag, or on a detached portion of rock, which the slightest exertion would apparently hurl into the valley beneath, will be seen one of these animals; but invariably far beyond rifle range. I made repeated efforts to accomplish the destruction of some of them, but failed so often that I

* Deep fissures, in which rivers run.

almost gave up in disgust. At length I was rewarded. The plan of operations which brought success was thus arranged. On a clear beautiful night I started from camp; all animated nature was hushed to sleep, excepting the tree-frogs and the "whip-poor-will" (a variety of goat-sucker), which kept inconstantly sighing out the melancholy note from which it derives its name. After a severe struggle, not unaccompanied by falls and bruises, I reached the first line of rocks; after resting, I again pushed upwards, till I thought I had gained sufficient elevation; so in my blanket I lay down in the most sheltered retreat I could find—for these elevated regions are cold—to wait for the break of day.

My plan, you will see, was to get above the game. From my own observation, and from remarks which I had heard, I concluded that these wary gentry dreaded danger only from beneath, and that, if I could obtain greater altitude than them, I should be successful. At length day broke—how long it is in coming under such circumstances!—and to my chagrin I was enveloped in mist, so dense that I could not see twenty yards from me; however, with the sun, the curtain of vapours rose, and rolled farther up the rugged slopes. With anxious and careful eye I surveyed every side; but not a sign could I behold of the creatures I sought. Determining on a return to camp, already I had commenced my descent, when, turning an angle, hundreds of feet beneath me, I saw three big-horns. One, the old gentleman of the party, stood on the edge of a precipice, the other two were lying down a few yards apart from him. There are moments of pleasure in a sportsman's life that leave a lasting impression on the tablets of his memory, such as death alone can erase : such was this scene. For possibly thirty minutes I gazed on the happy family. Still the veteran remained like a statue ; the affairs of the lower world were evidently of great interest, or its inhabitants were in his opinion a dangerous race who required much watching. Satisfied as far as seeing was concerned, availing myself of every obstacle that would shield me from observation, with the cunning and bloodthirstiness of the snake, I neared my victims. The stalk was an easy one, the face of the soil appeared formed for it. The point I had marked with my eye as the best place to shoot from was reached ; with care I protruded my head over it, and the figures of the tableau remained unaltered in position. As I raised my rifle, and glanced through the sight, I can still well remember that gentle monitor, conscience, whispering to me that I was about to commit a bloodthirsty deed, such as we men would condemn in the most wholesale manner if perpetrated by any of the inferior members of the brute creation. But still the admonition stayed not my purpose, nor disconcerted my aim. Against the ribs, at the back of the shoulder, I aligned my aim ; an imperceptible pressure of the finger was answered by a report, and with it a harmless animal had been deprived of life. As the father lay struggling on the ground, the wife and child fled—they to lose their guardian and natural protector, I to be no richer except by a few pounds of meat, and to be able to say I had performed such a deed.

But leaving the big-horns, I got to the beaver-dam in

due time, and, reaching the margin of the water, hid myself in a dense growth of willow. My presence was unknown to the community, for I had not been there more than a few minutes when two musk-rats (musquash) swam by. These pretty little animals are widely scattered over the American continent, and their pelt forms a considerable article of commerce. They are most expert swimmers and divers, with a quizzical expression of countenance which is both attractive and ludicrous. At maturity they are about the size of a half-grown cat, and, when obtained young, make admirable pets; however, their strong musky odour is much against their popularity for such a purpose. Still no beavers showed themselves, although I had been more than a couple of hours in my ambush, and I had lost several shots both at deer and ducks from my desire not to alarm the neighbourhood. However, patience meets its reward, and about four in the afternoon, a fine specimen of the beaver swam past, soon followed by a second and third. During the noonday heat doubtless they had been taking their siesta, and were now turning out for business or pleasure. Soon a dozen were in view, swimming to and fro, occasionally diving, but never remaining long under water. They appear to live a most happy life, the various members of the community being on terms of the strongest friendship with each other.

However, I did not see dam-building, or any of the skilful engineering qualities with which they are accredited, and I have long come to the conclusion that such rumours have emanated from the brain of imaginative persons. The dams which the beaver has the credit of building are thus formed: The spring and autumnal floods carry down immense quantities of timber, which in a bend or narrow place in the river form what the Canadian lumbermen call a choke—*id est*: the logs get jammed together, and, by the current's pressure by degrees become most firmly locked. The beavers which principally feed on the willow and osier, cut down the limbs that are within their reach; the leaves and tender shoots and bark are gnawed off for food, and the remainder floats down the stream, and by the pressure of the water is driven into the crevices between the larger logs, thus filling up intervening spaces, and forming an interlacing net-work. With continued accessions of small branches soon the whole becomes an immovable mass, and a permanent dam is formed, which so obstructs the water as to form, if the vicinity is level, an overflow. These extended sheets of water are called beaver-dams.

The first cool weather in autumn brought a flock of wild geese from the north, which in a few days increased to thousands. Ducks also made their appearance. All were in the finest condition, and far from wary. I observed not less than nine distinct species of *Anser*. To this may be added twenty-seven species of ducks, among which were to be found the genuine canvas-back, and a bird much resembling the eider-duck. Two species of swans are also numerous. On a cold day these various aquatic fowls might be seen going south in armies; with a rise in the thermometer the course of their legions would be reversed. Strange to say, they do not always confine their society to their own race; on one occasion

I counted five different species feeding together in the utmost harmony. But my residence in the parks was at an end. I had killed all the game I wanted, and could have killed more; and now in my own land I often sigh for the howling of the wolf, a serenade that would recall rough but true men—and dangerous, fatiguing, but happy days.

CHAPTER XXIX.

A HUNTING MISADVENTURE.

ALL those portions of the American continent which were settled by the French, and which have not since received an influx of emigrants from other countries, remain almost unchanged and unimproved. A few scattered log-dwellings and a few acres of cultivated land alone attest the presence of man.

How different are those parts which are colonised by the descendants of English, Scotch, Irish, or Germans! The forest rapidly disappears before them, and comfortable houses, smiling cottages, commodious barns, well-enclosed and highly cultivated fields, in a short space of time cover the entire surface of the land, which a few years previously was merely a wilderness.

Vincennes, in the State of Indiana, was settled by the French. The town has of late years become of some importance, because the Ohio and Mississippi Railroad runs through it; but down on the Watash River, not five miles off, is to be found the primitive forest, only here and there broken by the Frenchman's shanty and diminutive corn-patch. I once lived in this neighbourhood, for game was abundant, and fishing excellent ; but even with all these inducements, fever and ague were too prevalent, mosquitoes, jiggers, and ticks too abundant, to permit my stay to be of length.

In Vincennes there lived a gentleman who had once been an officer in the Prussian army. His love of hunting amounted almost to a mania, and he practised it at no inconsiderable expense; the better to indulge his foible, he kept a pack of—what shall I call them ?—certainly not hounds ; perhaps curs is the most applicable name. Well, K. had a good heart, but he had very bad sight, with a great aptitude for firing snap shots. Several times this little peculiarity had got him into trouble, for he almost killed one friend and severely peppered several others. At length his reputation became so notorious that no one could be induced to accompany him when in pursuit of game. This was to him a source of great grief, because he was of convivial habits, and loved dearly to show to the world what a wondrous clever pack he possessed, and how ably he hunted them. Soon after my arrival in Indiana, I made K.'s acquaintance ; and although numerous hints from outsiders were given me as to the uncertainty of life, more especially when with such a hunting companion, I would not be warned, but put down all as malicious scandal, and therefore refused steadfastly to be prejudiced against him until I had ocular demonstration of the fact.

One fine morning, in the month of November, I was awoke in that delightful portion of my sleep (which, with subalterns, is so often disturbed by the ration bugle when they happen to be orderly officers) by a most discordant to-tooing on an old cracked horn within the sacred precincts of my bed-room. Solicitations for ten minutes' respite for forty more winks, for sufficient time to recall my scattered senses, were of no avail; so, rather than insult my friend by throwing a boot at him—being a foreigner, I did not know how he might receive such a welcome—I sprang from my couch, made a hurried toilet and a hearty breakfast. Then, instead of indulging in an after-breakfast pipe, the most delightful of all the pipes of the day, I determined to lose no time, and postponed my smoke till I was in my saddle.

My mount was a pony, of about fourteen hands—handsome, good, and a great pet. I had not long possessed her, but already knew her valuable qualities so well that I would not have taken for her double the price she had cost me. Little did I imagine that this would be the last time I should cross my little mare.

The hunting-ground was reached, and this was our plan of operations. K. was to take the pack and make a drive down wind, while I remained by a favourite pass, which, previous experience told us, the deer were certain to traverse. In fifteen or twenty minutes after taking my stand, a solitary doe came in sight. With the most guarded caution she approached my ambuscade. Again and again she hesitated, but the yelping of the curs reminded her that her present course was scarcely optional—that she had either to go forward or run the gauntlet. At length her decision was formed. Forward towards my shelter she came. A few more strides brought her within easy range as to distance, but difficult for certain shooting from intervening brush. My first barrel, however, failed to do more than slightly alter her course; but as she passed me in more open ground, the left brought her tail down, caused her to spring several feet in the air, and stumble on to her knees, from which position she recovered, and was soon lost to view. Having reloaded, I quickly followed the hoof-tracks, and an old skirter of this pack of unmentionables overtook me; and ere he had gone a hundred yards, from the intonation of his voice, I knew he had reached the quarry. Hurrying up to the scene of action, I found the doe at bay, bidding the cur defiance with her feet, which she used most skilfully. The dog, however, was not to be beaten off. My presence gave him fresh courage; and after a couple of unsuccessful attempts, he laid hold, and I got a chance to blood my knife. Soon afterwards I brought up my pony; and, placing the carcass across his loins, made it fast to the D's in the cantle of the saddle. On returning to my post, I again heard the curs running, and evidently heading in my direction. The better to be able to use my gun, I made my nag fast to a sapling, and started at the double to cut off an angle; but I had not gone more than a hundred yards when, heading directly for me, I saw ten or twelve deer. Unfortunately they had seen me, and, sheering off to the left, passed close to the pony. To this moment I cannot tell the reason, but the little animal appeared suddenly seized with fright. She reared, backed, and struggled, till the bridle broke, and off she went in the direction of the hunt, bucking and kicking, evidently with the intention of divesting herself of the load. Soon she succeeded, for the saddle turned round, and the deer got underneath her belly, where it remained only for a few minutes before it was torn off. Not wishing to walk home, I hurried after the mare, but shouts and kind words were unavailing. The little blackguard, glorying in her freedom, only cocked her tail the higher, and accelerated her pace. Cogitating over my unfortunate predicament, I heard a couple of shots close at hand, and knowing full well that none but K. could have fired them, I pushed forward, and soon joined him. From his statement, he had just fired at a tremendous buck, with enormous horns. He was certain we should find him dead close by, and said that we had better wait till some of the hounds returned to assist our search. After an unusual amount of to-tooing, one of the so-called hounds joined us; but no exertion would induce him to take up the trail. "Very odd," said my friend; "the scent must be very bad to-day." "Very curious," said I; "my little mare has just passed this way; did you see her?" "No," he responded; "nothing passed but the buck I shot at."

A horrible thought crossed my mind—so horrible that I tried to banish it—no less than that the big buck was my pet pony. It was of no use. My suspicion I could not conceal, but K. was obdurate; the idea was absurd: could he disbelieve his eyes? ultimately we almost got to high words. No deer-track could I find, but that of the pony was plainly visible. The cur would not acknowledge the passage of game. There was no room for doubt; still I hoped that my friend had seen so badly that he had not held his gun straight. More of the mongrels now joined us, not one of whom could be induced to open. Several casts were made to the right and left, but without success. Farther into the woods we advanced in the supposed correct direction, when, to my horror and indignation, I beheld my pet writhing in a death-struggle! Even then my German friend swore by all that is high and low, that some one else must be the assassin, for that he had fired at a buck.

To waste my breath in argument with such a man was absurd. I therefore said little, but thought a great deal. At length a convulsive struggle indicated that death had relieved my unfortunate favourite. When I held a *postmortem* examination, the result showed me that not only had the charge of buck-shot been well placed for inflicting a mortal wound, but that a portion of it had ripped my saddle in numerous places. I fervently wished that the mare had been without a breast-strap, for then, when the saddle turned round with the deer, most probably she would have got rid of both; and I should have suffered only my loss in horseflesh, without the destruction of my saddle.

That day was the last which I passed shooting in the society of the Prussian, and, reader, take my advice, be most particular not to trust yourself in the company of careless persons carrying fire-arms! There is scarcely a sportsman, however young he may be, who cannot recall some terrible accident caused by such people.

Before leaving Vincennes, I will add a little shooting episode that happened on the grand prairie.

A Hunting Misadventure.

The morning dawned as wintry and wild as if my location had been in the Arctic regions, and, as travelling was out of the question, for I was *en route* to visit a friend, I was unwillingly detained captive for the day. A prairie farm in winter is far from an interesting domicile for any one, more particularly if confined to the house. After hours of inertness and a heavy consumption of tobacco, I decided to face the elements, draped in white, preferring to do so rather than roast over an uncomfortably hot fire in an uncommonly cold house.

Putting on as much clothing as if destined for picket duty before Sevastopol in winter, I went to the place usually selected by the prairie chickens (*Tetrao cupido*) for feeding. Here a portion of the corn had been cut, and still stood in shucks, with the ear on. Arriving at the spot, although the snow was flying with considerable violence, I saw several chicken on the wing, indications which I favourably construed into promise of sport. Selecting the most suitable stand, I was not long tasked with delay, for birds commenced passing in every direction: even those that I flushed only flew a short distance before returning. It appears to me that I never saw game tamer, my white dress over head and body approximating so closely to that of the ground that many, doubtless, supposed me to be anything else you like to imagine rather than a sportsman. Even some headed straight for the shuck behind which I stood, and, doubtlessly, would have alighted if they had not been disturbed by my movement or the report of my gun. One in particular, which came while I was loading, after being frightened from my shelter, went to the next stook and commenced feeding with perfect indifference. But such an ordeal is trying to a man's constitution, and to retain a sufficiency of animal heat required more vitality than I possessed, so that after an hour's work I was compelled to desist, with fingers stiffened, and toes nearly paralysed. For the last ten minutes, half the time was occupied in fumbling to place caps on the nipples, an amusement far from pleasant or soothing to an irascible temperament. Having obtained quite as many birds as I required, with satisfaction I returned to the influences of the fire, and uncomfortable shelter of the homestead.

Here, as in other parts of the world, I heard the old story of milk snakes, or of reptiles that suck milk from cows when in the pasture-fields, still I cannot believe these assertions, and I will give my reasons for my incredulity. In the first place, there are two distinct snakes called by this name in America, perhaps more. At the north end of Lake Simcoe, in Canada, a variety of snake, excessively numerous there, and which I should denominate the brown water-snake, was pointed out to me as a milk snake. In Southern Illinois, Iowa, &c., a handsome dark-blue snake, very rapid in his progression, and not at all unlike the common black snake, is always called a milk snake; and to both these varieties, in their different localities, is attributed the crime of sucking the cows. That the emigrant on Lake Simcoe or the squatter of the Western States believe this, there is no doubt; and like many yarns equally improbable, they are accepted, and handed down from father to son, without the idea ever entering their heads to examine whether it be possible. Both the brown and dark-blue snakes in question live principally on frogs, and their teeth are so situated that, when once they lay hold of their victim—if it is large and sufficient to open the mouth to its full extent—they can with difficulty leave go, without cutting or tearing. Now, a cow's teat is of such a size that, if the snake took hold of it, the milk could not be extracted unless the reptile closed its mouth for the purpose of suction, and scarification of the part would be the result. Cattle and horses have a great dislike to snakes, and will not at any time approach them voluntarily, being able to detect their presence by smell. On the western prairies, where stock-raising is the principal occupation of the farmer, snakes abound, many of them poisonous—such as the rattlesnake, mocassin, copperhead—still it is unusual, owing to this power of scent which stock possess, for an animal to be bitten. Now, can it be for a moment supposed that a cow would submit to an operation that would cause it pain, and that from a creature for whom it has the greatest antipathy?

However, the snakes to which my informant alluded are not the same as those I have mentioned. I cannot help believing that whether the reptile was white or black, short or long, this antiquated story is no more than a fabrication.

While shooting in this neighbourhood, the person who accompanied me, killed a very light slate-coloured snake, nearly six feet long, which he called a milk snake. My attendant assured me that this variety was in the habit of sucking the cattle. But it probably got the appellation from its colour, and imagination attributed to it the milking proclivities.

Snakes have long been the subjects of wonderful and impossible stories; for instance, in Texas and other portions of the United States, as well as at the Cape of Good Hope, a most dangerous description is said to exist, called the hoop-snake. It is supposed to be very long, and to have the greatest antipathy to equestrians, whom it pursues in the following novel manner: Taking its tail in its mouth, it forms a hoop, and follows its victim, trundling over rough and smooth ground with great velocity! How delightful to be coursed by such a customer! Everybody dislikes snakes; they have no friends; all will go out of their way to kill them: and, doubtless, they deserve much antipathy; but give a dog a bad name, and crimes and misdemeanours of which he is perfectly innocent will be saddled upon him. I very much believe the unfortunate snakes are saddled with numerous misdeeds of which they are entirely innocent, particularly that of sucking cows.

CHAPTER XXX.

CAREER OF AN EMIGRANT.

A SLIGHT sketch of the hardships and trials which the emigrant has to struggle through may be interesting to many. His life is not all sunshine, as some may imagine, and pleasure and rest are only obtained after days and years of toil and industry.

Let us suppose the emigrant to have reached Canada with his family, and arrived at the site where his destined home is to be; that he is a man of small means, in fact, with not more than sufficient to buy his seed-corn, procure one or two head of cattle and hogs, and sufficient provisions to last his household for, say, six months—the season, autumn. Just think what trials and anxieties are before this little coterie. First, the house has to be built. How many a hard blow, how many a blistered hand, aye, and how many a heartache must take place before that is accomplished! Hour after hour, day after day, the woods resound with the monotonous click of the axe; but how slowly does the work advance! for he knows not that sleight and skill that is so characteristic of the native American backwoodsman. At length sufficient space is cleared for the future domicile, enough trees have been cut and notched of which to compose it, and the light of heaven is no longer shut out by the foliage, but cheers the labourer and those depending on him, during their mid-day meal. If the emigrant have neighbours—and all who live within five or six miles are deemed so—he informs them that he is ready to "raise" his house. This summons is invariably attended to, and a dozen or more sturdy workmen soon have the logs placed in their respective positions, and before many hours the sides of the new dwelling are up. But supposing the settler has taken up land away off in the forest, far from where assistance can be obtained, he must make use of every available mechanical power that can be formed with axe and timber to place the unwieldy logs in their destined positions. This is slow and tedious work. The first roof is generally composed of bark, or black ash roughly riven into planks; this afterwards gives place to shingles, when time and experience have taught him how to make them. But logs are not all straight, and many are the openings in the walls which must be closed before winter sets in. This process is called chinking, and is performed by forcing into the crevices chips or rude laths of timber, which are afterwards daubed over with clay or lime. The fire is made on the floor, and the chimney, which seldom satisfactorily performs its duty, projects into the room, and is a composition of thin laths and clay or lime placed in alternate layers. Then the doors and windows are sawn out, a casing put in, and the emigrant's first home is fit for the reception of its future occupants. Tables, chairs, stools, and other interior necessaries are easily formed, but of course they are most primitive in construction, still they answer the purpose, or must do so until time has given the labourer a few good crops, or his character for industry and honesty has become established at the nearest store, when possibly credit can be obtained. But although the house is up, work does not cease. Morning, noon, and night, the axe must be at work, till sufficient space for the first crop is cleared. To accomplish this, not only have the trees to be felled, then cut into logging lengths, the boughs and limbs lopped off and piled, but possibly the surface of the land has to be underbushed. Those trees that, from their splitting easily, are suitable for rails are saved for that purpose, while the others, generally through the assistance of neighbours and their ox-teams, are drawn together, piled one upon another, and, when sufficiently dry, burned. A good burn can seldom be obtained till the timber has been cut at least a year, otherwise the logs have to be piled and repiled, fired and refired, before all are consumed. One thing you cannot get rid of, viz. the stumps. They must be seen to form a correct opinion of their unsightliness; and worse still, they take years to decay, some varieties of timber lasting an ordinary lifetime. During the process of firing, as logheaps are frequently built beside stumps, they get charred and blackened, and burnt into distorted shapes, such as an imaginative mind can fabricate into all sorts of spectres. When the land is fit for cultivation, it has to be fenced. This generally is done by splitting ash, hickory, or elm into rough rails from ten to twelve feet long, which are placed upon the ground, the end of one rail resting on that of the other, like a succession of letter W's, till sufficient altitude is obtained. Rail-splitting is laborious work, and many a day's pounding with a gigantic mallet, there called a beetle, has to be done ere a large log is dismembered into rails of the requisite size. A fence of brush is sometimes temporarily employed; but it is dangerous to trust your maiden crop to such a fragile enclosure. Cattle and hogs are not easily excluded from such tempting food as green wheat or corn. You may not possess any stock yourself, yet your neighbours possibly do, and as the habits of all are very erratic in wild land, the unfortunate settler who has trusted to a brush fence may awake in the morning to find the result of all his labour and toil, the hope of his family for next year's subsistence, totally destroyed. To prepare the land after clearing for the reception of the first crop, the ashes that remain after burning are well scattered, when, if oats or wheat are to be sown, they are generally scattered broadcast, and not unfrequently harrowed in with a branch; when a better implement is not obtainable. If the emigrant have sufficient funds to purchase a yoke of cattle, when he has learned to drive them—no easy matter—they will be found most useful; in fact, the first purchase that all should desire to make is a pair of these useful animals—without them I should deem it almost an impossibility for any one to succeed; but patience and determination will accomplish much. In the meantime, how are the family living? what is their food? Pork, flour, and corn-meal—and, believe me, there are few articles of human diet that are capable of being less metamorphosed by human ingenuity than the aforementioned. Occasionally a duck, grouse, or even deer may fall to the settler's gun, and if in the vicinity of water, fish may easily be captured. But as a rule, those who devote themselves to field sports become idle and improvident, and lose caste among their neighbours. A garden has also to be prepared, although the variety that it will produce is not great ; still, potatoes, cabbage, and pumpkins will be found acceptable additions to the table ; beans also can be grown, and are a useful article of diet, combined with pork, for those who have to work hard in winter. In Yankeeland, pork and beans is a standing dish, and, when properly cooked, is not to be despised. In choosing the situation of a residence, high ground should be selected, more especially if on the margin of a river or lake. Freshets will occur on the breaking up of winter, and it is far from agreeable or conducive to comfort to have one or two feet of water in the interior of your dwelling.

Sheep can seldom be kept when the country is new, for they form so great an attraction to wolves that these gentry are almost certain, sooner or later, to pay them a visit, which will not cease till they have destroyed all. Poultry, if unmolested, will do well ; but the skunk, grey fox, and several varieties of hawk, are apt to be troublesome in their attentions to them, more especially to the young birds and chickens. If one or two of these marauders be occasionally shot and hung up in a conspicuous place as a warning to their mates, beneficial results have frequently followed. A disagreeable incident that too frequently occurs is the straying off of the milch cattle and working oxen. Sometimes they will be gone for days; to obviate this as much as possible, the ringleader of the mischief, which is generally an old cow, has a bell attached by a leather collar to her neck, the tinkling of which can, in calm weather, be often heard half a mile off. With what pleasure have I listened to the tinkling of a cow bell! Every note speaks of your approach to man's dwelling, and probably a resting-place; nothing but the deep voice of the honest watch-dog speaks so emphatically to the wearied and perhaps homeless wanderer.

Although timber is abundant, to provide the necessary quantity of fire-wood for a family's use is no small labour, for it has to be cut into lengths and split, and afterwards piled within easy access of the door, and the consumption of fuel during a Canadian winter is sufficient to astonish the uninitiated. A good fire always gives an air of comfort; therefore few regret the toil that is required to produce it. As grain cannot well be used without grinding, the more accessible and close the settler is to a mill so much the better; for many trips will have to be paid to it, and bush-roads are not generally to be commended for affording the means of rapid transit. If the mill be on navigable water, a sale may possibly be found for some of the settler's choice timber, thus bringing an ever-welcome supply of cash to his pockets. Considerable outlay can be saved by the manufacture of your own sugar: this takes place in the spring of the year, when the warm sun causes a thaw during the day; the sap then commences to ascend the trees, and by tapping or notching the bark of the hard maple, and driving in a spill underneath where the incisions are made, a bucket or even more liquid may be obtained in the course of a few hours. The sap is then collected from the rude buckets into which it has fallen, underneath the respective trees, and is deposited in a large kettle to boil; thus, by degrees the moisture evaporates, the remains first becoming molasses, ultimately sugar. Care must, however, be taken that the whole does not boil over; this can be obviated, if a person cannot be spared to be in constant attention, by hanging a piece of fat pork over the caldron so as to fall a few inches beneath the level of the rim; on the sap boiling up to the pork, it will cease to ascend any further. Making maple sugar is laborious work when done on an extensive scale, for the trees and fire require constant attention, and collecting sap and possibly having to carry it a hundred or more yards, through slush and brush, is no joke. In the second season sundry outhouses are generally erected, for we will suppose that the emigrant is at length the possessor of a few head of stock. Among these, pigs will probably be found the most remunerative, for they require little or no food, except in winter, and become fat on what they obtain in the bush; instead, therefore, of having to purchase your supply of pork, it is provided at home—a saving of the most expensive item in a family's expenditure. The only drawback to the propagation of pigs are their predatory habits and their liability to be eaten by bears. The former proclivity it is almost impossible to prevent; the latter misfortune must be guarded against by the destruction of bruin, a feat well worth the trouble, for the hide will sell for a considerable sum, and the flesh make an acceptable addition to the larder. If a bear once obtains a relish for pork, day after day he will desire to gratify his appetite, and a young porker must pay the penalty. I have even known bruin come to a pig-sty that had a covering of logs, roll them on one side, and carry off a victim. In fact, I shot a bear one night in the very act of committing such a depredation. The pig-sty was under the gavel window of a shanty in which I was spending the night. The father and mother had gone with a grist to the mill, which was some distance off, and consequently they were not expected back till the morrow. The pigs had been for half an hour unusually noisy, when one of the children rushed into my rude dormitory and informed me that a bear was endeavouring to get into the hog-pen; taking my gun, I went to the window before mentioned, and there I saw Mr. Bruin, for the moon was bright, lifting or rolling on one side the logs that had been placed as a protection against his inroad. Soon he had made an opening and descended into the pen, returning immediately with a porker, when I gave him his quietus in the shape of an ounce and a half of buck-shot fired within three or four yards.

The persons who emigrate to Canada must be prepared and able to work hard, to labour night and day for some years—more particularly if they go where land is cheap; by that time, what with the influx of emigration, and the increase of population, farms advance in value, for markets are established nearer at hand, and the stamp of civilisation becomes more apparent. The first years have been spent in struggling and toiling to make both ends meet; but during the latter years plenty of food, if that constitutes happiness, is obtainable. With some classes this is all that is desired; with the educated, and those who know the advantage of mixing with others than boors, I feel confident in saying, their aim in life points a little higher.

COURTEOUS READER,—We have now made the tour of the world together. We began our sporting experiences in Scotland, when, as a mischievous school-boy, I slaughtered an unfortunate robin, but by degrees I learnt to fly at higher game, and before I left my native land, the antlered deer had fallen a victim to my gun. Going abroad, we have fished in the blue depths of the Mediterranean; we have hunted with a pack of staunch British hounds on the soil of sunny Spain; we have climbed the rocky hills of North Africa in pursuit of game. Thence, we have passed to India, beyond all question the favourite *locale* of the military sportsman, for there ranges the tusked wild boar, whom we scorn to slay with bullet, but rejoice to spear; there crawls the repulsive alligator, and there lurks the stealthy tiger. In China the game we followed was of a more inoffensive description, but in the Flowery Land, and still more in the fascinating islands of Japan, we were repaid for the comparative tameness of the sport by the interesting character of the country and the people. Then we crossed the greatest ocean in the world, the mighty Pacific, disembarked at the Golden Gate, the land of auriferous wealth and American enterprise, penetrated into the fastnesses of the interior, encountered the buffalo and the grisly bear amid the illimitable prairies, or the sheltered valleys of the Rocky Mountains, and, lastly, turning our faces homewards, we have traced the slow progressive stages whereby the Canadian backwoodsman teaches the gloomy and barren wilderness to smile with abundant harvests of golden grain. Reader, we must now part; I thank you heartily for your companionship, and wish you a sincere farewell!

THE END.

www.ingramcontent.com/pod-product-compliance
Lightning Source LLC
Chambersburg PA
CBHW032104230426
43672CB00009B/1637